Legendary

The Story of the 2019 San Francisco 49ers

by Akash Anavarathan, Eric Crocker, Kyle Posey,
Alex Tran, Kyle Breitkreutz, and Mark Saltveit

Edited by Mark Saltveit

Palindromist Press
Portland, Oregon
www.legendary49ers.com
© 2020

ISBN 978-0-9718714-3-4
First edition, published February 7, 2020
Cover design by Rick Hawkins.
Chapter text is by Mark Saltveit unless otherwise noted.

To my dad, Carl Saltveit, who taught me about football and many other things.

-- Mark Saltveit

I'd like to give thanks to my wife Styvie Crocker for putting up with my football obsession.

-- Eric Crocker

I dedicate this book to my dad, mom and brother. The three of them continue to motivate and support me in my passion of writing about sports – specifically the 49ers. I wouldn't be able to do this without them.

-- Akash Anavarathan

To my fiancé for always being supportive of me and allowing me to create content about the sport I am passionate about. Hopefully my daughter Harlow can read this when she is older and know that she can do anything she puts her mind to.

-- Kyle Breitkreutz

Table of Contents

1. No Divas, No Stars, No Problem 1
2. The Scheme 15
3. Building the Roster 33
4. September 77
5. October 93
6. November 135
7. December 151
8. Playoffs: Divisional Round vs. Minnesota 165
9. NFC Championship vs. Green Bay 173
10. Super Bowl LIV 183
11. The Future 195

Contributors 203
References 205

Chapter 1. No Divas, No Stars. No Problem.

Who is the star of the San Francisco 49ers?

Maybe it's tight end George Kittle, who set the NFL record for tight end receiving yards in just his second season. But if he's a star, it's because of his outsized personality, his love of pro wrestling and his readiness to give hilarious quotes to any reporter within 100 yards.

On the field, though, Kittle likes to block every bit as much as catch passes. Maybe more. That's one reason why he was available in the fifth round -- the Niners are one of the few teams in pro football heavily focused on blocking.

Nick Bosa could be the star of this team. After all, he was the number two overall draft pick, and he's made an immediate impact as an edge rusher rarely seen from any rookie. But Bosa is just one part of defensive line that rushes as a team, backs each other up and celebrates each other's successes. And he's just fine with that.

Normally, the quarterback of a winning team becomes a star almost by default. He has the ball in his hands on every play and makes all of the crucial pre-snap and post-snap decisions to make the offense run.

Jimmy Garoppolo, though, is quietly efficient; he's happy to hand off all day if it's working, or to throw short passes in stride for big gains after the catch. He steps up exactly as much as needed -- to throw aggressively downfield or run a quarterback sneak on 4th and 1 -- and not a bit more.

As a result, a lot of pundits dismiss him, compared to flashier QBs hucking it downfield all the time. You don't want to pick him in fantasy football; his statistics are unimpressive.* But like Kittle and Bosa, all he really cares about is winning, and he's pretty good at that.

As a starter, Garoppolo is 23-6; that's the best winning percentage (79.3%) among active quarterbacks, ahead of Lamar Jackson (79.2%), Patrick Mahomes (77.8%) and Tom Brady (76.9%). [1]

That's even more impressive when you consider that his team was 2-14 the year before he arrived, and had a 1-10 record when he took the helm midseason. After Garoppolo tore his ACL in 2018, those same Niners were 3-10 during his absence.

The reality is that the 49ers do not have a star. They are a true team, focused on winning, supporting each other and having fun while kicking ass.

These guys do the dirty work. Running backs and wide receivers are as happy blocking as having the ball in

---

* This is not completely fair; Louis Riddick pointed out that Garoppolo was the only NFL quarterback who was in the top 5 in passing completion, touchdowns, and average yards per completion in 2019. (https://twitter.com/LRiddickESPN/status/1221197912987897857)
But fantasy football points get all the attention, and for that you need yards and TD; you want to draft a QB on a team with a bad defense and no running game.

their hands. They prefer squads of skill players, not one marquee diva — who can get injured or develop an attitude.

Stars make the ESPN highlights, but teams make goal-line stands and shut down their opponents on third and fourth down, as the 49ers did all season. Teams can run down your throat with several different RBs, and score 37 points while throwing only eight passes in a playoff game. The only 49ers "player" you want in fantasy football is their defense.

It's a strategy

We all love stories of humble, hard-working underdogs who triumph against cocky, big-name talent: Rocky, the Miracle Mets, the 1976-7 Portland Trailblazers defeating Julius Erving's 76ers.

But this team is no "Bad News Bears." General Manager John Lynch and head coach Kyle Shanahan know that the star approach, diva-chasing, is a dangerous and flawed strategy that, in the salary cap era, only works in the short run if at all. They're building not just a playoff run, but a budding dynasty (in the 49ers tradition).

Look at the Los Angeles Rams, who mortgaged their future by trading draft picks for big name veterans, and signing marquee free agents. It got them to the Super Bowl in 2018, where they were humiliated by New England and then collapsed the very next year, not even making the playoffs.

When you build around big names, you end up with little depth. Those stars are vulnerable to injury, and defensive coordinators can scheme around them. A stud cornerback such as Jalen Ramsey can shut down almost any star receiver. But when you face a platoon of WR2s instead of one WR1, your star CB can only cover one of them. And if he gets injured, your secondary is doomed.

Blue collar skill players, elite linemen

The Niners have built a roster full of fast, unheralded running backs and reliable receivers, each with different strengths and weaknesses. These are the chess pieces Kyle Shanahan loves to play with, exploiting matchups and the element of surprise. And his team has weathered a bad run of injuries, always having someone else who can step in.

It's an old cliché that great football teams are built in the trenches. A lot of coaches pay lip service to that idea, but Lynch and Shanahan *do* it. And the simplest evidence of that is where the team puts its resources.

One reason there are no big-name stars on this team is that linemen don't get much attention, even when they are excellent. But that is where San Francisco has put its resources. Two tweets (by ESPN's Nick Wagoner [2] and Josh Dubow of the Associated Press [3]) tell the story. There are literally no skill players who were first round draft picks on this team.

> **Josh Dubow**
> @JoshDubowAP
>
> The only first round pick with a pass catch or run in Shanahan's 3 years is Joe Staley with catch for -5 yards vs Denver in 2018
>
>> **Nick Wagoner** @nwagoner · Jan 15
>> Need more evidence of Kyle Shanahan and his coaching staff's work putting together an offense and developing players?
>>
>> With a win Sunday, #49ers would be the 7th team to reach the Super Bowl without a pass, rush or catch from a former first-round pick, per @EliasSports.
>
> 9:50 AM · Jan 15, 2020 · Echofon

Joe Staley is the team's left tackle; he caught a deflected pass once to prevent it from being intercepted.

It's a very different story with linemen, though; eight of the 16 offensive and defensive linemen on this roster were first round picks, and center Weston Richburg was taken in the 2nd. And yet, reporters seem to be surprised when they win in the trenches, week after week.

To be fair, the 49ers were focused on building the lines on both sides of the ball before John Lynch was ever a GM. Besides Staley, the team already had first round picks in Arik Armstead (2015) and DeForest Buckner (2016), as well as offensive guard Joshua Garnett (2016) when Lynch showed up -- and Garnett didn't even make the roster in 2019.

Lynch then drafted DE Nick Bosa, DT Solomon Thomas and OT Mike McGlinchey with his three initial first-round picks (the second, third and ninth picks overall, respectively), and traded for edge rusher Dee Ford and OG Laken Tomlinson.

Clearly, it paid off. Kyle Shanahan's first playoff game as head coach came against the Minnesota Vikings, who surrendered only 26 sacks in the entire 16-game regular season -- 5th best in the NFL. San Francisco sacked Kirk Cousins six times in this one playoff game, once by each of the team's five first-round defensive lineman except Bosa -- who sacked him twice. And the Vikings couldn't move the ball.

Block first, score points later

This is a team where physicality and blocking is a priority, for every offensive player, without exception. That includes every wide receiver, the punter (who was flagged for unnecessary roughness), and quarterback Jimmy Garoppolo, who pancaked Minnesota linebacker Anthony Barr in the playoffs.

That's the attitude that fuels this team. The scheme is built around its best blockers; aside from the linemen, George Kittle and Kyle Juszczyk are the wild cards who make it impossible for defensive players to predict any play, and San Francisco hit its roughest patch in 2019 when they were both out, injured.

It's not macho posturing. That's how the offense works as a team. Every player learns what every other player does on each play, for two reasons; first, because Shanahan runs the same plays with different players getting the ball, and second, so that everyone knows how to block downfield, without even looking.

That's a big part of why this team gets so many yards after the catch, and so many explosion runs that go for 15 to 50 yards where other teams might get 6 to 8 yards out of the same hole.

Humility

In a profession of elite talent where confidence and brashness are common, this Niners team has a hard-working humility that keeps them honest, yet frees up a loose, fun-loving ease -- maybe because they don't take themselves too seriously. In the run-up to the Super Bowl, players like Deebo Samuel, Kendrick Bourne and Emmanuel Sanders were often seen dancing or goofing around during lulls in practice, or while taking the stage at mass media events.

At practice on Friday, two days before the biggest game of their lives, several players pulled a prank on their coaches by swapping jerseys to mix up their numbers. Nick Bosa switched with Jimmie Ward, and Kyle Juszczyk swapped with Tevin Coleman, as did tight ends George Kittle and Levine Toilolo. Coach Kyle Shanahan said:

> *"They surprised us with it. They are loose and feeling good, and they had fun with it. We'll see how it is when we watch film."* [4]

Even Richard Sherman, the fierce veteran sage with all the gravitas and history, shares this attitude, telling David Lombardi of the Athletic that he chose the 49ers in part because of the relaxed atmosphere that coach Shanahan creates:

> *"I have fun. I like music at practice. I like to hang out and be relaxed in meetings. I don't like the stressful environment in football."* [5]

That may surprise you, since Sherman is clearly the leader of the defense, and known for finding (or, arguably, inventing) slights and beefs with opponents to fuel his drive. And I would certainly not recommend pissing him off, if you can help it.

But on his own team, he is studious, hard-working and supportive of all his colleagues. He told David Lombardi that

> *"... we're all on the same level. That's something I learned in Seattle. There's no hierarchy of players. Because as soon as you have that, you don't have a great locker room.*
> *Everybody has to feel that they're even, even if they're not [by some measures]. Everybody should be approachable. And I think it starts with Jimmy [Garoppolo] and myself.*
> *Because once we don't make ourselves above anybody, then how can anyone else?"* [6]

This attitude starts at the top. Defensive Coordinator Robert Saleh described his head coach this way at a January 23, 2020 press conference:

> *"The most underrated thing that I think is misunderstood about Kyle [Shanahan] is his humility, to know when he doesn't have the answer. A lot of people might look at Kyle as somebody who is, 'This is my way, it's, I already know. You don't need to tell me.' But when you actually sit down and talk with him, if you can present a case, he just wants, he wants answers that are right for the organization.*
>
> *He's not looking to force his opinion just because it's his opinion. So, he's got a tremendous amount of humility to be able to listen to everyone's opinion so that the right decisions are made for the organization, so it can continue to move forward.*
>
> *The combination of him and John's humility, I really, really believe is why this organization is where it is today."*[7]

This is a team where the players don't care about statistics, don't care about personal glory, don't care about being "the man" as long as together, they are "the men."

The lack of attitude also extends to admitting mistakes and knowing what you have to learn. While preparing for the Super Bowl, star rookie wide receiver Deebo Samuel was asked for an "untold story" about this season. He said:

"I never thought I was gonna learn the playbook, or get on the field. It was so complicated for me at first. [You have to] know what everybody got going on. Honestly, I'm still learning to this day to be honest with you."

Clearly he learned a lot. But this kind of directness and honesty about failings is what gets players to keep improving.

Another key is not obsessing over personal achievements. On January 24th, Richard Sherman retweeted a bit of video, where George Kittle (mic'ed up) was caught talking to Emmanuel Sanders on the sideline, after a play in the NFC Championship Game against Green Bay.

The two best receivers for the team were amazed (but not unhappy) about a game plan that included only 8 passes the entire game -- and had San Francisco leading 27-0 at halftime.

Kittle: "Man you ever been in a playoff game [before] where you had zero catches?"

Sanders: "No. It happens."

Kittle: "Who gives a {unintelligible}??"

Sanders: "Yeah, I don't."

Kittle: "I just want to win, dude."

Sanders: "Exactly." [8]

Even better, the lack of divas means more glory for everyone else.

Running back Raheem Mostert made a point, after touchdowns, of handing the ball to one of his offensive linemen so he could spike the ball in the end zone. After all, he wasn't going anywhere unless the "big uglies" opened up holes for him.

The cover of this book is a picture of just such an occasion, Laken Tomlinson spiking the ball after a Mostert TD.

During Super Bowl media week, Mostert explained why:

> *"The O-linemen don't get enough appreciation for the things they've done. They go out there and do the grimiest of grimiest jobs, setting those blocks, protecting the quarterback. ...That's hard work, and I appreciate it. So, let them celebrate, give them the moment.*
> *If they want to spike the ball, and all the guys want to spike the ball, they love it. That's just appreciation, and I appreciate them for the things that they do.*
> *I gave Joe [Staley] the ball, man, against Seattle, and he just went crazy. He looked [down] at it, and said 'Oh yeah, you know what time it is.' They live in that moment, and I'm happy I can do something for them."* [9]

This attitude goes all the way up to owner Jed York, who charted enough planes to fly over 1,500 49ers staff members and their spouses out to Miami for the Super

Bowl. York told Cam Inman of the San Jose Mercury News:

> *"We're taking a lot of people. We wanted to make sure that our entire staff had the opportunity to go."* [10]

You could say there are no stars on this team, or you could say that their humble, hard-working attitude makes everyone a star.

Kwon Alexander: Legendary

The Niners' biggest free agent signing in 2019 was middle linebacker Kwon Alexander, a 2017 Pro Bowler who tore his ACL after six games of the 2018 season.

The Niners signed him to a big 4-year, $54 million contract, and he immediately solidified the linebacking core alongside overachieving second-year LB Fred Warner and the outstanding rookie Dre Greenlaw. He even coined a name for his unit -- the Hot Boyzz.

Alexander's speed and passion energized the defense, and his pass coverage skill was the secret sauce in the drastic improvement in the team's pass coverage, from one of the NFL's worst in 2018 to 2nd best in 2019. [11] Rookie star Nick Bosa called Kwon

> *"... the MVP of our team. He's the energy, all the time. It's kind of hard for 16 games, every single day, to bring the passion and have fun with it. If he's there, we have no choice but to have fun."* [12]

Kwon also gave this book its title with his positive attitude. On October 31st, he tore his pectoral muscle during a Thursday night game against the Arizona Cardinals, and the team declared him out for the rest of the season. When he came out of his surgery to repair the injury, clearly feeling the effects of his medical treatment, Alexander recorded an Instagram video describing his surgery as "legendary." [13]

Some fans thought it was a funny moment, perhaps a description of his pain medication as much as the surgery itself, but this has been the linebacker's motto for a long time, at least since he tore his ACL in 2018. As he told Matt Maiocco of NBC Sports, [14]

> *"I don't like to use the word G-O-O-D. 'Good,' [because] I'm trying to be better than that. So I use that ('legendary') to get my mindset where it needs to be.*
> *[After my injury, the] thing was to stay focused and keep your mind straight because a lot of people get down in those situations. I'm just telling myself to stay focused, keep praying, and I'm going to get back to myself even better. That was the main goal."*

His attitude helped bring this young team together and vault it to the elite level, and the word "legendary" became a prophecy that becomes more real with every game.

Chapter 2. The Scheme

It's easy to give a simplistic description of the 49ers offensive and defensive schemes under the current coaching regime: a lot of outside zone runs (OZR) mixed with play-action passes on offense, and a Seattle-style cover 3 zone on defense.

But San Francisco's schemes are anything but simplistic.

Once-predictable reliance on cover 3 was replaced in 2019 with lots of pre-snap motion, disguised looks, and other schemes (notably quarters coverage and a variety of 2-high safety looks.)

On offense, the OZR plays mix in with nearly every other kind of run: power, zone reads, RPOs (run-pass options), swing passes and jet sweeps.

Steven Ruiz of USA Today's "For the Win" catalogued the following run plays in the NFC Championship Game against Green Bay: [15]

> *"I'm sure I missed one or two, but here are all the run concepts the 49ers ran in the NFC title game:*
>
> *Outside zone*
> *OZ toss*
> *OZ split*
> *OZ RPO*
> *Wind-back zone*
> *Trap*

Counter
Power
Sweep RPO
Inside zone
IZ split
Lead
Toss"

Then there are tendency breakers, counters, traps and fakes for each of these. For example, if a defense overplays the outside zone too aggressively, Shanahan has counterpunch plays to punish them for it, like F-counters or an outside zone with a fullback wind back like the one Matt Breida ran on the first play from scrimmage against Cleveland. [16]

Juszczyk faked like he was going to lead block to the outside, then turned back inside to take out Olivier Vernon, as Breida also cut inside and burst through the line, running past safety Damarious Randall for an 83-yard touchdown. [17]

Kyle Shanahan's offensive scripting is elite, but the system isn't easy to learn; you have to master a lot of details. Matt Ryan was much less effective in his first year running it, but blossomed in year two when Atlanta went to the Super Bowl.

Jimmy Garoppolo did well running a stripped down version of the scheme when he took over mid-year after his 2017 trade, but he looked less comfortable running the full system in the first three weeks of 2018 (his sixth, seventh and eighth games in San Francisco).

After his injury gave him a year of studying the system's intricacies, and talking directly with Mike Shanahan (the retired originator of this scheme), he seemed fully comfortable in it 2019.

Motion, and more motion

Furthermore, Shanahan uses pre-snap motion constantly, forcing the defense to reveal their strategy and giving them every opportunity to misread the play, or get pulled out of their run fits.

The 49ers have led the NFL in pre-snap motion every year that Shanahan has coached them, and the percentage keeps rising, from 66% in 2017 (per PFF) to 70% in 2018 and 79% in 2018. [18]

Each pre-snap shift forces the defense to reveal itself three times:

  1) their response to the initial formation,
  2) whether anyone follows the shifting player (a coverage indicator which shows whether it's man-to-man or zone coverage), and
  3) their reaction to the final set.

And Shanahan sometimes puts two different motions into a single play.

Connections between the plays

Coach Shanahan does not just collect random, interesting plays or drawing up completely new ones to surprise defenses. Each play has a connection to one he has called in the past, often with a little modification designed to throw off defenders, exploit their reactions, reveal defensive strategy or set up another, future play.

The best defenders in the NFL (such as Richard Sherman) study tons of their opponents' game film, so that they can react instantly and intuitively when the same situations and plays arise in a game. Coaches devise their game plans from that same study and analysis.

Shanahan has tendencies, and he knows that defenses know what they are, but he uses that knowledge against them - breaking his own tendencies, or setting up defenders to think "Oh! I recognize this play, I'll cheat over to where it's going" -- only to have it be a disguise for a different play that punishes their adjustment.

Versatility helps. Every skill player can catch passes, and everyone blocks on runs. Even the smallest receivers block, and even the fullback and tight ends can motion into the slot for a quick slant or run a wheel route out of the backfield with surprising speed.

This allows him to hide his signature plays from defenses by running them from different initial formations, followed by a shift, or by running the same play but with different players.

He knows that players and coaches associate a play with the skill player who carried the ball; if the man they are looking for is away from the action, they don't expect it. Against the Saints, for example, Shanahan took plays that worked for TE George Kittle, and ran them with receivers Kendrick Bourne and Emmanuel Sanders -- scoring touchdowns. [19]

Of course, eventually defenses will get suspicious and not react as quickly to plays -- but that's also a win for the 49ers, who have assembled the second-fastest roster in the NFL (barely behind Kansas City). Even a bit of hesitation is enough for a Raheem Mostert or Marquise Goodwin to blow by you.

Oscar Aparicio of the Better Rivals podcast noted another nuance, in a podcast with Eric Crocker. [20] Defenses rely on "tells" (or "reads") to predict where a play is going, anything from how wide or tight splits are to which side of the quarterback a runner lines up on, or even the fact that a receivers fiddles with his gloves before the snap.

Shanahan knows these tells and then deliberately falsifies them, lying with his players' position, motion, and probably some revealing indicators that you and I have never noticed. Football players succeed at the NFL level playing on what we call "instinct," but in many cases that's just what we call their ability to instantly process a bunch of tiny little clues.

They don't even need to be able to list them, as long as they look at an offensive formation and can guess where it's going. Shanahan wins by knowing what keys that defenses react to, and falsifying them by making the players keyed on "lie" with their movements.

Fullbacks and the I-Formation

The 49ers run a lot of old-fashioned I-formation (with a quarterback, fullback and RB in a straight line behind the center). The advantage is that the play is able to go in either direction, without losing any blocking power or tipping off the defense.

Schemes don't work in the abstract, on a chalkboard or Surface Pro tablet; a coach needs the right talent to execute them. Kyle Shanahan has made the fullback a foundation of his offensive scheme, and Kyle Juszczyk is probably the only player in the NFL today who's versatile enough to do everything this offense calls for him to do.

21 NFL teams have fullbacks, but many are used sparingly, and Juszczyk is the only one currently who is enough of a receiving threat to force defenses to account for him. If they don't, he can and will catch a 50 yard pass to flip the field or score. The Harvard graduate has soft hands, solid speed and toughness after the catch, in addition to rivaling George Kittle as a skilled and enthusiastic blocker.

Each year, he picks up more yards through the air (reliably 250-325) than most fullbacks gain in their entire career, combined. The next best FB pass targets are the Patriot's James Develin and Buffalo's Patrick DiMarco (who was Shanahan's fullback when both were in Atlanta). But they average only around 50 yards a year.

Using the fullback as more than a blocker is part of San Francisco tradition, hearkening back to Bill Walsh's offense (an important precursor of Shanahan's) and to an earlier fullback with the same number 44, Tom Rathman.

Rathman totalled 2,684 receiving yards in 9 NFL seasons, numbers very similar to Juszczyk's (though he was a much better runner with 2,020 yards in his career, and even returned five kickoffs).

> *"The fullback is the most critical part of our passing game, because he's the most difficult to handle." -- Bill Walsh* [21]

Watch the long runs that the Niners break so often. Many times, you will see Juszczyk lead block into the hole, taking out a linebacker or defensive back who's trying to fill that gap, with Mostert or Breida just an inch behind him, "hugging the block" before exploding past the second level into the open field. The chemistry and timing that Juszczyk has worked out with the runners is incredible.

Shanahan aims for total unpredictability, and with Juszczyk in the game, defenses have no idea if the play is a run, pass or RPO. Against a base defense aimed at stopping the run, Juszczyk can motion out wide or fake a block and run a wheel route out of the backfield. If they focus on pass defense with a sub package, he can punish them as a lead blocker.

That's not all, either. In high school, Juszczyk played quarterback in a Wing-T scheme that included some triple option concepts, and Shanahan has used that experience by featuring him in a speed option play, which the team ran against Kansas City in 2018 [22] and the Saints in 2019. The fullback takes a handoff and can toss or keep, based on his read. Who knows? Maybe they'll include a pop pass option the next time they run it.

In many of today's NFL offenses, fullbacks have been replaced by sets with two tight ends on the line of scrimmage, one on each side, which makes it tough to load the box and play single safety. If you do, the tight ends can break immediately for pop passes or run four verts.

The problem is that it's very difficult to get both TEs blocking for the same run play, since they can only block defenders on the side where they're aligned. You could put them next to each other, but then their blocking angles are difficult at the second level, [23] plus and the defense knows which direction the play is going.

Shanahan, in contrast, can send his fullback to either side, and often runs plays where Juszczyk starts in one direction (to get the defense flowing there) before abruptly turning to head the other way. He can start blocking and fall back into pass protection, or take off downfield.

With passing games dominant, teams are stocking their rosters with more mobile, smaller, faster coverage-oriented defenders. Few teams have linebackers or strong safeties who can withstand a full speed fullback coming through that hole. The Niners can just overwhelm them, even if a team stays in its base defense (as Green Bay did in the playoffs).

At the same time, 49ers can motion Juszczyk out wide and have him run deep, without substituting (or allowing the defense to substitute). If a cornerback covers him, Shanahan has created a mismatch elsewhere, probably with a linebacker covering a wide receiver. If a linebacker covers him, the 49ers have just lightened the box for possible runs and given the fullback a good chance of beating his man one on one.

No tight end running sideways from the line of scrimmage or a step back could hit those blocking angles, or have that much momentum. Even if two tight ends are side by side, they're not able to get same angles that a blocker running in the same direction as the running back can get, plus you've tipped your hand on the play direction. [24]

New developments

One weakness of Shanahan's 2017-2018 offense was his red zone offense (a problem that Jim Harbaugh shared at the beginning of the decade). But in 2019, the coach made important strides.

In 2018, the Niners were dead last in the league for red zone touchdown rate, at 41.18%. They improved to 54.29% (21st) in 2019, and higher than that (63.64%) in the last 3 games of the regular season, which would have been a top 10 conversion rate if sustained all year.

Kittle has helped. In the red zone, as analyst Ted Nguyen notes, the 49ers like to send him on a "swirl" route, which looks like a corner route until he abruptly spins to the inside and posts up the defender in the end zone, like a basketball player -- specifically, like a power forward posting up a point guard. [25] Very few defensive backs are big enough or tall enough to out-muscle him in this situation.

An important trend, driven by new talent, is emphasizing physicality as well as speed on this roster. Perhaps because of George Kittle's success with yards after catch in 2018, Shanahan added players such as Deebo Samuel and Jalen Hurd who are not just fast, but brutal in overpowering would-be tacklers. And it worked.

Hurd didn't play due to injury, but Samuel emerged as a star, and more physical receivers such as Kendrick Bourne moved ahead in the rotation over, say, Dante Pettis. And it worked: more than 55% of the team's receiving yards came after the catch, compared to 48.4% for Kansas City.

The defensive scheme

It's impossible to assess the 49ers defensive scheme without looking at the talent they added: Nick Bosa and Dee Ford transform the pass rush, and make each other more effective. With Dee Ford on the field, the 49ers don't need to blitz; they have the best four-man rush in the league, and the extra coverage defender gives them more time to get home.

This was immediately apparent in game one against Tampa Bay as the defense produced four takeaways and three sacks, while holding the Buccaneers to under 300 yards of total offense. While he gets less attention for it, Bosa is also very stout against the run. Even when the play goes away from him, his speeds often enables him to take down a runner or quarterback from behind.

Likewise, new players Dre Greenlaw and Kwon Alexander turned the linebacker position from a weakness to a strength, one that deserves some of the credit for the team's new-found power in pass coverage.

The 49ers also "added" two key players who were already on the roster, because they healed from injuries. Richard Sherman played through 2018 but he wasn't himself, and we saw in 2019 how good -- even great -- he can still be in his thirties. And Emmanuel Moseley was a revelation and a complete surprise, since the 2018 undrafted rookie free agent (or UDFA) had barely been promoted to the active roster during his rookie year when he was lost for the season, injured.

But it would also be a mistake to attribute their dramatic improvement to improved talent alone.

49ers defensive coordinator Robert Saleh changed his approach dramatically, perhaps under the influence of Joe Woods, the 49ers' new passing game coordinator who had led Denver's stingy secondary for four years.

In the past, Saleh has stayed almost religiously committed to Pete Carroll's single high, cover three system, which became predictable. In 2019, he mixed up the looks -- playing a good amount of quarters coverage -- and did a lot to disguise the coverage pre-snap, including motions that mirror Kyle Shanahan's frenetic use of motion on offense.

From game one in Tampa, analyst Ted Nguyen observed, Saleh seemed to be using concepts straight out of Vic Fangio's system, giving the offense the same initial look (with two deep safeties) on most plays — but the defense then might rotate into a different coverage, or stay with the two-deep. [26] The defensive backs might be playing quarters, Cover 2, a combination of both or they could even rotate into a Cover 3 zone.

Not surprisingly, Kyle Shanahan (who loves to keep his opponents guessing) was impressed. Speaking to reporters the day after the Tampa Bay game, he said:

> *"I thought [Saleh] did a good job. He mixed it up, kept them offbeat. Guys didn't know where we were always lined up. He mixed the coverages up, moved the D-linemen, stunted them some, rushed some straight, mixed in some pressure. I thought he did a real good job. Anytime you can keep the quarterback and the play-caller off-base, it helps the players have a chance to get turnovers."* [27]

He even mixed up one of the most famous elements of his scheme, where Richard Sherman sticks to the offense's right side no matter what. That's still the norm, but Saleh (or Woods) now has Sherman shadow a stud receiver from time to time, picking crucial moments.

In the divisional round of the playoffs against Minnesota, for example, Sherman stuck with Adam Thielen when he moved into the slot on a play at the SF 13 with 0:44 left in the first half, a crucial third-and-11. [28] Kirk Cousins got sacked and lost eight yards, limiting Minnesota to a field goal.

Arguments about whether the pass rush or pass coverage is more important miss the point. In a great system like Saleh's, each makes the other stronger -- leading to coverage sacks, and pass rush-pressured interceptions.

San Francisco's assistant coaches

Kyle Shanahan and Robert Saleh made crucial adjustments to their schemes in 2019, which kept them ahead of opposing play-callers, and they deserve all the credit that they get. The Niners were lucky that Saleh didn't get hired away at the end of the year as the head coach of another team.

At the same time, it's too easy for journalists to focus on the guy at the top, and miss the crucial contribution of the assistant coaches in building a team.

For Shanahan's offense, two long-time coaches never get enough attention for their good work: Bobby Turner and Katie Sowers.

Bobby Turner coached at Ohio State before joining Mike Shanahan's staff in Denver, where he stayed for 14 years until he joined Shanahan's staff in Washington in 2010. He moved to Atlanta (under Dan Quinn and offensive coordinator Kyle Shanahan) in 2015, and followed Kyle to San Francisco two years later.

Now 70, he has a low media profile for no good reason at all. Turner has been turning no-name, unheralded college RBs into productive NFL backs for 25 years; what does a guy have to do to get some recognition?

In his current position, he has been astoundingly successful getting production from a series of undrafted backs: Matt Breida, Jeff Wilson, Jr., and Raheem Mostert (who had been just a special teamer kicking around the league).

Katie Sowers was a football star in the Women's Football Alliance; she

> *"helped lead the U.S. to the women's world title and gold medal in 2013. In a semifinal win that year, Sowers intercepted five passes, returning three for touchdowns."* [29]

Sowers interned with the Falcons when Kyle Shanahan was OC, and again with San Francisco, before getting hired as a full time assistant coach -- the second woman ever in football, and the first openly LGBT coach in any of the U.S. men's professional sports leagues.

While she's still very early in her career, players from Marquise Goodwin to Jimmy Garoppolo rave about her attitude and knowledge of the game. Shanahan says

> *"She did a really good job for us in Atlanta. She's done a real good job here. ... She's a hard worker. You don't even notice her because she just goes to work and does what's asked and because of that she's someone we would like to keep around."* [30]

In contrast to these quietly efficient offensive assistants, Robert Saleh brought in two entirely new coaches who made major, high-visibility contributions: Joe Woods and Kris Kocurek.

While Saleh did shake things up a bit, using more quarters coverage for example instead of sticking with Cover-3 so rigidly, it was probably the influence of these coaches more than his own adjustments that catapulted a Niners defense that was frankly pretty bad to become the best or second-best in all of football.

Joe Woods has coached football for 26 years, and came to the NFL in 2004. He joined Denver's staff in 2015 and won a Super Bowl his first year; his teams were top five in pass defense by various measures every year he was there, and he was promoted to defensive coordinator in 2017 when Wade Phillips left.

As defensive coordinator, Woods improved the team's run defense just as dramatically, as Denver leapt from the 28th-best run defense in 2016 to 5th in 2017, and 3rd best overall defense.

Denver freed him to interview elsewhere after hiring a defensive coordinator, Vic Fangio, as their head coach. The

49ers were lucky to snap him up as passing game coordinator and defensive backs coach.

With no new players (aside from Jason Verrett who played four snaps, then got injured), the team that set the all-time record for fewest interceptions in 2018 gelled into the first or second best passing defense in the league, throughout the 2019 season.

Not surprisingly Woods was hired away as a defensive coordinator (in Cleveland) as soon as the 2019 season ended. Let's hope that his staff took a lot of notes during his brief stay.

Kris Kocurek, a defensive tackle himself, was a defensive line coach for nine years in Detroit and one in Miami before coming to San Francisco.

For all their first round picks, the 49ers DL had underperformed for years, often getting pressure but not finishing sacks. Kocurek immediately strengthened them in several ways with one common feature -- working together as a unit, rather than freelancing for big marquee plays or personal statistics.

Everyone expected a better pass rush with the drafting of Nick Bosa and the trade for Dee Ford, and Kocurek delivered that. But he also developed the line into perhaps the NFL's best at stopping crucial short-yardage plays -- 3rd and 2, or 4th and 1 -- which is just as important for getting your defense off the field.

As the Niners terrorized opposing quarterbacks, he also handled adjustments well. For example, after mobile quarterbacks and the screen game torched his men several times midseason, he modified the rushing attack to emphasize containment and to neutralize screens.

Just look at the difference between the first and second Seattle games in 2019. On November 11th, Russell Wilson picked up 53 yards on 6 scrambles, including an 18 yard gain. In the rematch, he only got 29 yards on 8 carries -- and his biggest gain was 5 yards.

Chapter 3. Building the Roster

Of course, the best schemes in the world won't help if you don't have the right NFL-level talent to execute them.

Owner Jed York learned his lesson from years of conflict between GM Trent Baalke and a succession of coaches; it doesn't matter how great a player the GM picks, if the coaches won't play then, or can't use their talents. So the rebuilding of the franchise in early 2017 started with the search for a coach and a GM who could communicate and collaborate, fusing together a unified vision of strategy and the precise players who can execute it.

He chose wisely. As Richard Sherman told David Lombardi,

> *"I don't think there's anybody that can stop Kyle when he has the personnel that he's picked and put into spots, and I don't think there's anyone that can beat [defensive coordinator Robert] Saleh when he has the personnel that he's picked and put into spots."* [31]

But when coach Kyle Shanahan and GM John Lynch took over the 49ers in January 2017, the cupboard was bare. The firing of coach Jim Harbaugh was followed by massive exodus of talent, like a mini-Syrian refugee crisis.

It wasn't just that free agents Frank Gore, Michael Crabtree and Mike Iupati signed with other teams. Five players *retired*, including relatively young contributors such as linebacker Patrick Willis (30), offensive tackle Anthony Davis (25) and rookie LB Chris Borland (25).

General manager Trent Baalke did not do well restocking his larder, either. Of the players selected in the 2015 draft, only the top two picks (DL Arik Armstead and safety Jaquiski Tartt) and punter Bradley Pinion (in the 5th round) really contributed. If anything, 2016 was worse: first round pick DeForest Buckner (another huge University of Oregon defensive lineman) and rotational DE Ronald Blair, a 5th round flyer from Appalachian State, were the only ones who stuck.

To be fair, Lynch inherited a few good players, starting with perennial All-Pro left tackle Joe Staley, Buckner, Armstead and Blair. Jimmie Ward, a talented defensive back who could play both safety and cornerback, struggled with broken bones -- fans joked that he should be forced to drink more milk -- but impressed when healthy.

Safety Jaquiski Tartt was strong as well, and Chip Kelly's best move in San Francisco may have been signing Raheem Mostert, a kick return specialist who came very close to making Kelly's first roster in Philadelphia in 2013.

Mostert bounced around several NFL rosters before landing with the depleted Niners. The coaches gradually developed his talent, first on special teams where he became the league's best gunner on punt coverage, and then as an explosive running back.

But those seven players -- along with long snapper Kyle Nelson and marginal tight end Garrett Celek -- were the only survivors of the Baalke era on the entire 2019 53-man roster.

Two Rookies

The team's new leaders were rookies, too. GM Lynch was a hard-hitting safety turned TV commentator. While he was well-liked as a person, there were people around the league who weren't thrilled about him vaulting to the top in his first front office job, without working as a scout or at least a director of player personnel first.

Kyle Shanahan had been an assistant coach forever (since 2004), and grew up as the son of longtime NFL coach Mike Shanahan, but this was his first head coaching gig. Furthermore, he had just lost Super Bowl LI to the Patriots as the Atlanta Falcons' offensive coordinator, blowing a 28-3 third quarter lead in what many consider the worst choke in Super Bowl history.

He was widely criticized for not running out the clock in the second half, though to be fair it was the defense that gave up 31 unanswered points, and that was not his responsibility. But for all his aggressiveness, his offense did not score another point during that stretch, which definitely was on him.

One striking development during 2019 was Shanahan's development of a potent "four minute offense," able to run out the clock with a strong run game when he had the lead.

Character

We've already talked about how this team has no divas and no stars. You don't get a true team like that by accident. John Lynch and Kyle Shanahan have designed the roster for teamwork, and owner Jed York is behind them all the way.

York is very young -- he was just 28 years old when he was appointed the 49ers' president (and later CEO) by his parents, who owned the team. It's not a secret that he has faced a great deal of criticism during his tenure, especially in the dark days in 2015-6 after GM Trent Baalke fired Harbaugh (with Jed's support).

But he remembers the glorious days when his uncle Eddie DeBartolo Jr. made the Niners the best team in football, if not the best franchise in all of sports. The days of Joe Montana and Jerry Rice and Tom Rathman, when the 49ers won 5 Super Bowls in 14 years.

And, 8 days before his second Super Bowl, York told reporters that the defining moment for the Shanahan - Lynch regime was when they cut a talented but troubled (and troubling) player, Reuben Foster.

> *"I love Reuben. I wish he was still here. We gave Reuben opportunities. We've given a lot of guys opportunities, but we set our limit and said if we can't fix this, we have to move on from a talented player... this is a first-round pick in our first year. And we moved on from it, and it was hard.*
>
> *We could have justified not moving on from it,*

> *there are other people that have been in worse situations than what Reuben has been in. But we knew where we had to be and I think that to me, if you look at a defining moment for those guys, and I think that's a defining moment for the culture of this team of, we are team first and we got your back first."* [32]

There's no room for me-first players on a championship team, and even being messed up is a way to make it about yourself. After a very checkered (but productive) college career, Foster was arrested first on gun and drug charges, then a second time for domestic violence. The circumstances were murky -- earlier domestic violence charges against Foster were dropped after his girlfriend recanted her allegations -- but when he was arrested seven months later for slapping the same woman, the team was done with him. [33]

Lynch made intelligence, hard work, humility, versatility, physicality and speed mandatory for his player acquisitions -- as opposed to a famous name, production in college, or playing for a big-name football program. And his values have paid off dramatically.

He also has worked closely (and communicated very clearly) with coach Shanahan about the exact traits he needs players to have. Given his unusual system, that lets the team grab players who don't fit the standard metrics sought by other teams -- and work perfectly in San Francisco.

Let's talk about speed for a second. No NFL team says they want slow players, but Shanahan and Lynch go further. Wide receiver Marquise Goodwin placed 10th in the long jump at the 2012 Olympics, and plans to compete again in 2020. The team's top running backs (Mostert, Breida, McKinnon and Coleman) have all run a 4.41 40-yard dash or faster; Mostert hit 4.39. [34] That compares to the average for NFL running backs of 4.59.

Unusually, the Niners' wide receivers tend to be slower (but bigger and more physical) than their running backs. Their primary targets are TE George Kittle (4.52), Kendrick Bourne (4.68) and Deebo Samuel (4.48). Fullback Kyle Juszczyk ran a 4.77. Even slot receiver Trent Taylor only managed a 4.63.

Recent acquisition Emmanuel Sanders is the only receiver who's as fast as the running backs (4.41), and it's no surprise that he quickly became Jimmy Garoppolo's favorite target on 3rd down, and in tight window situations. (The NFL average for wide receivers is 4.48.)

It's a good guess that Shanahan has thought this all out as a strategy, to hit defenses with faster running backs and bigger, more physical receivers than they are used to. He likes to zig when everyone else zags. And to be honest, his passing targets are usually wide open when the ball comes their way due to brilliant play design, so speed is less important than when you are bursting through a hole in the defensive line and trying to outrun defensive backs.

2017: complete rebuild

Lynch set about cleaning house drastically in his first year as general manager, waiving or releasing 39 players and signing 29 veteran free agents.

One of his shrewdest signings was cornerback K'Waun Williams. The promising young third-year slot CB was suspended for two games and fined by Cleveland, after they disputed his ankle injury. Williams got a second opinion by an expert at the Cleveland Clinic that confirmed that he had bone spurs and needed surgery, but the team was unpersuaded and cut him at the end of training camp.

The NFL has done a very good job of building parity into the structure of the league, with shared TV revenues, the salary cap and the draft. That makes the Cleveland Browns' record of continuous failure all the more amazing. It takes a lot of bad choices to miss the playoffs in 20 out of 21 years, and this was a good example of how they did it.

Chicago claimed K'Waun off of waivers one day later, but he failed his physical due to -- wait for it -- bone spurs. Williams got his surgery and missed the 2016 season. Lynch signed him in February and picked up a starting cornerback for free, as Williams beat out two veteran slot corners (Will Redmond, who started four games for Green Bay in 2019, and Keith Reaser).

Another interesting transaction came right at the end of training camp: trading a 5th round pick for offensive guard Laken Tomlinson, a 2015 first round pick for the Detroit Lions who they considered a flop. He missed week one cramming on the Niners' intricate playbook, but the Jamaican has started at left guard ever since.

Some of Lynch's free agent signings didn't pan out, including high-priced vets DT Earl Mitchell (4 years, $16 million) and LB Malcolm Smith (5 years, $26.5 million), but the team picked up two key pieces: ultra-reliable kicker Robbie Gould, and fullback Kyle Juszczyk, a Harvard grad who can use his own name as a password.

Kyle Juszczyk

Lynch handed Juszczyk the highest contract for a fullback in NFL history, $21 million total over four years, and he has been worth every penny.

It is not an exaggeration to say that "Juice" is the key to Shanahan's scheme, along with tight end George Kittle, because they give San Francisco the ability to execute any play, from a sledgehammer run to "4 verts" (known on the playground as "everybody go out long") with the exact same players. Both of them can block very large defenders with evident pleasure, line up anywhere on the field, or streak down field for a sure-handed reception and manhandle defensive backs for yards after the catch.

That's how you keep a defense guessing. Few NFL teams even carry fullbacks anymore, because most of them are only good for blocking and an occasional changeup run. The moment you put a traditional FB in the game, the other team knows it's not a pass play, and they offset any advantage you gain by putting in their base (run-stuffing) defense.

Juszczyk, though, is both a great lead blocker and a legitimate deep threat receiver with surprising speed and soft hands (76.9% completion rate, and 10.6 yards per completion in his three years in SF). If you don't account for him on a passing play, he can easily score on a 50-ish yard reception, as he has done in each of his 3 years in San Francisco.

Juice was an All-American tight end at Harvard, but converted to fullback since the NFL has no interest in 6'1" tight ends. He's been so successful that he's sparked a resurgence of fullbacks in the NFL, with an emphasis on other pass-catching road graders.

The 2017 draft

Thanks to the team's 2-14 record under one-and-done coach Chip Kelly in 2016, Lynch was picking second in the draft. Frankly, though, he didn't do much with that opportunity, at least not in the early rounds.

He did pull off a great trade, picking up three extra draft picks in return for letting the Bears move up one place to get QB Mitch Trubisky. It's hard to understand why Chicago would do that -- it seems obvious that if Lynch was willing to even discuss the trade, he had no intention of taking Trubisky -- but Lynch wisely didn't ask too many questions.

But his first few picks were not well spent. The rookie GM had met Solomon Thomas -- the Niners' third 1st-round defensive lineman in three years -- while taking a class at Stanford, but the 6'2" DT was a stretch as the #3 overall pick. He has spoken publicly about the psychological challenges of dealing with his sister's suicide, and by his third year he was no longer starting. Lynch may have let his personal fondness for the young man cloud his football judgment.

Lynch also traded away a fourth-round pick to move up three spots and take LB Reuben Foster -- a talented mess of a player -- at the end of the first round. Foster showed flashes of his potential before a series of arrests on drug, weapons and domestic violence charges led the Niners to waive him in 2018. He hasn't played a snap since.

Backup QB C.J. Beathard (3rd round) did not perform well after starting quarterback Jimmy Garoppolo got injured in 2018, falling behind UDFA Nick Mullens in the depth chart, and RB Joe Williams -- who Kyle Shanahan pounded the table for -- was a complete bust in the 4th.

The other 3rd round pick -- Ahkello Witherspoon, a tall and talented cornerback -- has alternated between brilliant and very shaky. But oddly, Lynch got much better players in the later rounds with much lower picks, and nabbed three key skill players who weren't drafted at all. A year later, it felt like he should just trade down all of his top picks for 10 or 20 fifth rounders, because that's where Lynch is a genius.

No one illustrated this more than tight end George Kittle, a fifth round pick who set the NFL record for TE receiving yards in his second season (2018) -- and he's even better at blocking. Teams overlooked him because his college team, Iowa, rarely passed to anyone. We can speculate that C.J. Beathard, Iowa's quarterback alongside Kittle, might have tipped off the Niners to his tight end's hidden receiving ability, and if so, he was worth a third round pick just for that crucial piece of information.

Lynch is typically modest about this franchise-changing pick. Just before the Super Bowl, he told Albert Breer: "We weren't too smart either, we waited until the fifth round."[35] And his point is well-taken. All draft picks are gambles to a degree. People say that Bill Belichick was a genius for drafting Tom Brady at the end of the fifth round; but if he really had any idea how good Brady was, he would have taken him in the first round, not the fifth.

Lynch also nabbed Trent Taylor (a very productive slot receiver when he's not injured) at the end of the 5th round, run-stuffing nose tackle D.J. Jones in the middle of the 6th, and hot-and-cold safety Adrian Colbert in the 7th.

Among undrafted players, QB Nick Mullens (Southern Mississippi) beat out Beathard eventually for the backup spot behind Garoppolo, RB Matt Breida (Georgia Southern) proved an explosive running back and solid receiver, and WR Kendrick Bourne has evolved into a key part of the 49ers' receiving corps, arguably their best red zone threat.

The Elegant Tank

For two years, Lynch and Shanahan had very few wins to show for their losses. The 2016 49ers were 2-14 during Chip Kelly's one year as coach, but they were even worse in 2017 before the Jimmy Garoppolo trade. That team was 1-9 when The Handsome One took the helm.

And yet, the team was clearly improving. Losses were close, and morale was strong because everyone could see what they were building. The coaches gave promising rookies and UDFAs such as Matt Breida and Raheem Mostert lots of playing time, and many of them proved very talented.

San Francisco set a record for close losses in 2017 -- five in a row by three or fewer points [36]-- and I coined the term "The Elegant Tank" to describe the approach. [37]

Typically, tanking is a bad idea because you get the stink of losing on you. Athletes are competitive by nature, and if they aren't, you don't want them. So losing a lot kills morale.

Beyond which, you're asking players to put their bodies on the line with every play; why would they do that if they know you are trying to lose? It takes real elegance to not destroy team spirit through a bunch of losses.

But the reality remains, that losses get top draft picks which make a team better. Before the Super Bowl, even Jimmy Garoppolo's joked about how his knee injury turned out to be a good thing, because the 49ers got the second overall draft pick, which turned into Nick Bosa and Deebo Samuel in rounds one and two.

That took a bit of additional luck, even so. The Niners got the #2 pick with a 4-12 record, because only Arizona had a worse record, and they won a couple of tie breakers with other 4-12 teams. But in 2017, a 4-12 record only earned the 5th pick. Four teams were 3-13 or worse.

And one tiny little trade....

For all that frenetic rebuilding, John Lynch's most significant addition may have come via a mid-year trade. And I don't mean getting a 5th round pick from the Jets for struggling cornerback Rashard Robinson, who was subsequently arrested in New Jersey for careless driving and possession of "THC infused Peanut Budda Buddah Candy." [38]

Jay Glazer has reported that, during the summer of 2017, Lynch tried to convince Bill Belichick to trade him New England's backup quarterback, Jimmy Garoppolo -- and that when he was denied, he asked for Tom Brady instead.

> *"Belichick just said, 'What did you just ask me?"* Glazer reported. *"(Lynch) said, 'I'm asking if you'd trade us Tom Brady, (since) you said Garoppolo is off-limits. (Belichick) said, 'Did you just ask me if I'd trade Tom Brady? ... Did you just ask if I'd trade the greatest quarterback of all time?' And John said, 'So is that a no?'"* [39]

Garoppolo had value as insurance against an injury to the 40-year-old Brady, but he let people know that he wanted to be a starter wherever he ended up, and that wasn't going to happen in New England.[40] So just before the trade deadline, Belichick called Lynch back to see if he was still interested in trading for Jimmy G - at the cost of a second round pick.

He was -- in fact, Lynch was prepared to offer more than that. After the trade was completed, San Francisco won all five games that Garoppolo started at the end of the 2017 season.

2018: hitting his stride

Four important players came to the Niners via free agency in 2018, none more important than cornerback Richard Sherman. This nemesis of the Niners was unceremoniously cut by Seattle after he tore his Achilles tendon, and signed with San Francisco almost immediately.

Sherman had a long dinner meeting with Kyle Shanahan that involved the two of them recalling -- off the top of their heads -- precise details of the various times that Sherman had messed with Shanahan's passing offense in different games with different clubs - Houston, Washington, and Cleveland. Sherman, a Stanford graduate, is one of the shrewdest analysts of the NFL passing game on or off the field, which makes him perfect for Kyle Shanahan's team.

Sherman negotiated his own contract without the use of an agent, bringing criticism (from agents -- who would have guessed?) that his incentive-laden contract was lopsided in the Niners' favor.

What they weren't considering (aside from the commission payment he got to keep) is that Sherman crafted a contract designed to light a fire under his own ass, one where he bet on himself and could make a lot of money only by being the best.
What else would you want him to do? Asking for guaranteed money even if you suck does not seem conducive to championship football.

With $4 million extra from his incentives (including bonuses for playing time, and being picked to the Pro Bowl and All-Pro teams), Sherman earned $13 million in 2019 -- more than he ever made in Seattle, where he never bested $11 million. [41]

RB Jerick McKinnon was an explosive running back with great receiving skills, seemingly a perfect piece for this offense. But he tore his ACL in the 2018 training camp and reinjured it a year later. After two expensive years without playing a snap, he may never suit up for San Francisco before they release him -- especially since the team has Tevin Coleman and three highly successful undrafted free agents on inexpensive contracts.

Center Weston Richburg was another key free agent pickup, though. At his previous job in Atlanta, Shanahan's offense did not take off until the Falcons acquired center Alex Mack in free agency. His complicated offensive scheme needs a mobile and highly intelligent center to make it hum. In 2018, Richburg struggled as he worked through injuries, but entering 2019 he had regained the top form that convinced Lynch to sign him.

To complement Richburg, the team also signed veteran guard Mike Person, who plugged a hole at guard. Like his fellow guard Laken Tomlinson, he's the type of offensive lineman who is doing well when you never hear his name, and that has largely been the case during their time in Santa Clara.

The 2018 Draft

If the 49ers' 2017 picks were successful mostly in the lowest rounds, Lynch's second draft was impressive from top to bottom. All nine players chosen are still on the roster and contributing, at least as depth or special teams players, and that's unheard of.

First round pick Mike McGlinchey is excelling as the team's starting right tackle, and LB Fred Warner has been a very productive team leader at linebacker. Even as a rookie, he wore the helmet with the green dot, indicating he had the one earpiece to hear instructions from the sideline and quarterback the entire defense.

Second round pick WR Dante Pettis notched an impressive 467 yards and 5 touchdowns in his rookie season, but 2019 has been more complicated, as we'll see. Shanahan pushed his team to be much more physical in his third year, including lots of blocking by wide receivers on run plays, and Pettis does not seem to fit in nearly as well as Kittle, Deebo Samuel, Emmanuel Sanders, Kendrick Bourne or even 5'9", 185-pound WR Marquise Goodwin -- who aroused no suspicion lining up alongside McGlinchey at the end of the offensive line on one play against Cincinnati, and blocking for a bit before leaking out unmarked for a 38-yard touchdown.

The rest of the 2018 picks have all developed into valuable depth pieces, though DL Kentavius Street has barely been healthy enough to play. Street, DB Tarvarius Moore, CB D.J. Reed, S Marcell Harris, and DT Julian Taylor are all in the rotation, and the second 7th round pick -- WR Richie James, 240th overall -- finished 2019 as the team's leading kick returner.

Lynch had continued success with undrafted rookies, too. Ross Dwelley has made some plays as a depth tight end, and Jeff Wilson, Jr. was yet another fast, unheralded running back that has been successful for the Niners.

But the most important UDFA in 2018 was cornerback Emmanuel Moseley, a talented guy who went undrafted probably because he is 5'11". A high school quarterback, he ran a 4.42 40-yard dash at his pro day, and played four years against the best college receivers as a cornerback at Tennessee, an SEC school.

The Niners cut him at the end of the preseason and stashed him on the practice squad (with a higher-than-normal salary, equivalent to that of a roster player). Moseley was called up on November 1st and played just three snaps on special teams against the Oakland Raiders before hurting his shoulder and going on Injured Reserve for the rest of the year.

He ended his rookie season almost completely unknown, even to the team's biggest fans, but that would not last long.

2019: topping off the tank

By Lynch's third year, the talent level of the 49ers had risen sharply, and fewer unknowns made the roster. Two of the most interesting were obscure blockers with unusual backgrounds who were essential in helping the team survive injuries to their most important offensive linemen.

Ben Garland

Garland was a defensive lineman at the Air Force Academy, then had two years on the NFL's very obscure Military Reserve List after he signed with Denver. (That means that he practiced with the team but couldn't play, and they didn't have to pay him anything.)

After that, he was signed to Denver's practice squad and started taking offensive linemen reps "as a joke," after he mocked offensive linemen for having an easy job. [42]

The studious, hardworking two-way lineman eventually made it onto Denver's active roster, playing occasional snaps both on offense and defense, then signed with

Atlanta when Kyle Shanahan took over as their offensive coordinator.

Garland once sacked Russell Wilson for a safety, and had a quarterback hit on Tom Brady in the 2016 Super Bowl, but had started a total of only seven games in his career (all at offensive guard) when he signed with San Francisco in April 2019, at age 31.

When center Weston Richburg was lost for the season in mid-December due to a kneecap injury, Garland took over. Never mind that he had never played center before; he's a quick study.

Not only did Garland protect Garoppolo against inside rushers, he led an offensive line that absolutely dominated in the playoffs, as the Niners ran and ran and ran. PFF (Pro Football Focus, a service that grades every player on every play) rated him as the second best 49er in the playoff victory against Minnesota, ahead of George Kittle. [43]

Daniel Brunskill

The other great find on the NFL scrapheap was Daniel Brunskill, from the AAF. The what? Exactly.

The Alliance for American Football was a new, eight-team professional league that began play on February 9th, 2019 -- and went broke less than two months later.

That was enough time for 49ers scouts to spot Brunskill during his eight games as a tackle for the "San Diego

Fleet," and invite him to training camp. He had been a walk-on tight end at San Diego State, then spent a couple of years on the Falcon's practice squad but never made the active roster. Brunskill won a spot on the Niners roster by playing all five offensive line positions with skill and athleticism.

When the team's swing tackle (Shon Coleman) got injured in training camp, and then both starting tackles were knocked out mid-season, Brunskill got his chance. He was excellent -- better than sixth-round draft pick Justin Skule, certainly. Now Brunskill is in the mix as a possible starting tackle when Joe Staley decides to retire.

Free agents

Lynch made smart moves to extend key players including Raheem Mostert, Mike Person, special teamer Mark Nzeocha, and Jimmie Ward. But by this point, improving the Niners' already strong roster generally required some real capital, either a large free agent contract or trading a draft pick.

His most controversial off-season move was placing the team's franchise tag on kicker Robbie Gould, one of the NFL's most reliable field goal kickers. (Gould made 72 of 75 FGs in his first two years in San Francisco).

Conventional wisdom holds that kickers are interchangeable and basically free, so franchise-tagging one was by definition too much money; yet a lot of games are lost on missed field goals. After he was tagged, on

April 26, Gould (who was 36 at the time, and presumably near the end of his career) requested a trade to his home of Chicago, but he agreed to a four-year, $19 million extension with San Francisco on July 15th.

Lynch signed three well-known free agents. Jason Verrett was an elite cornerback for the Chargers with a horrible record of injuries; he managed to play only 25 games in 5 years. Lynch signed him to a one-year contract for $3.6 million, somewhere between a wild gamble and a reclamation project. True to form, he played only four snaps (and got roasted on those) before his season ended on the injured reserve list. Oh well, it was worth a try.

Running back Tevin Coleman was the backup RB for Kyle Shanahan's Atlanta teams, but he clearly has untapped potential with his combination of size and speed: 6'1", 210 pounds, 4.39 speed in the 40 yard dash, and a capable receiver in the passing game. He was quiet most of the season but stepped up to play a big role in the playoffs with 22 carries for 105 yards against Minnesota.

The biggest coup in free agency was middle linebacker Kwon Alexander. The high-energy overachiever, a 4th round pick who immediately started at middle linebacker for the Tampa Bay Buccaneers, was a PFWA rookie of the year and a 2017 Pro Bowler.

He tore his ACL after six games the following year ,in 2018. At the ripe old age of 25, he became the grizzled veteran in the Niners very young and very talented linebackers room, alongside Fred Warner, Dre Greenlaw and Azeez Al-Shaair. (See separate articles on Greenlaw and Al-Shaair.)

Trades

Lynch picked up two key players in trades, in return for all of the team's second, third and fourth round picks in 2020. Before the draft, he acquired Dee Ford came from the Kansas City Chiefs for a second rounder, adding punch to the Niners' underachieving pass rush and insurance in case Arizona drafted the player the Niners wanted, edge rusher Nick Bosa.

Mid-season, at a time when the team's wide receiver corps was struggling, Lynch nabbed veteran Denver wide receiver Emmanuel Sanders. He made an immediate impact, solidifying a receiving group alongside tight end George Kittle and receivers Deebo Samuel and Kendrick Bourne. Sanders' playoff experience was also a plus on this very young team; he had played eight postseason games in four different years with two teams, and won a Super Bowl ring with Denver in 2015.

Was he good value? That's a complicated and interesting question. Sanders' contract expires at the end of the season, which is why Denver was happy to get something in return for the remainder of his contract. He only cost the Niners $6 million for the rest of 2019, a great value for a wide receiver of his talent, but he'll be a free agent in March. [44]

The Niners gave up their 3rd and 4th round picks in 2020, and got back Denver's fifth round pick (which will be the 15th selection in that round). But their 4th round pick will be at the end of that round, so they might lose only about a half-round of value on that swap.

And if they let Sanders walk in free agency, San Francisco will likely get a 3rd round compensatory pick back, getting back the 3rd round pick they traded. If so, they'll give up a 4th round in return for a choice in the round where John Lynch found George Kittle, Trent Taylor, and Dre Greenlaw. Not bad.

The 2019 draft

I'm not going to lie. There were some disappointments in the 2019 draft.

One of the most exciting prospects was 3rd round pick Jalen Hurd, a former running back who converted to wide receiver and has the physicality to play as a tight end. He only played in two preseason games before going on the injured reserve list with a back injury, though, and never recovered enough to play.

Of the last three picks (TE Kaden Smith, tackle Justin Skule, and CB Tim Harris), only Skule made it into a regular season game and the results were not good. Harris was injured in training camp and essentially given a redshirt year, but at 6'2" and 197 pounds, it will be interesting to see how he performs next year.

The rest of the picks were solid, though. Some draft analysts will never believe a punter is worth a 4th round pick, or any draft pick at all frankly, but Mitch Wishnowsky has performed well, especially at avoiding touchbacks (just 2 all year) and limiting returns (a combined 131 yards).

He also handles kickoff duties, taking some pressure off of field goal kicker Robbie Gould, and destroys kick returners [45] in a way that's rare among NFL punters and kickoff specialists, but maybe more common in his native Australia. Against Carolina, he got an unnecessary roughness penalty for crushing Reggie Bonnafon after 35 yards of a punt return.[46]

WR Deebo Samuel (2nd round) was outstanding, one of the most physical wide receivers in the NFL even in his first year. He racked up 802 total yards and 3 touchdowns, adding 159 rushing yards on just 14 carries (an astounding 11.4 yards per run).

Linebacker Dre Greenlaw, a fifth round selection, stepped up in a huge way after Kwon Alexander got injured and proved to be an outstanding playmaker. In the close loss to Seattle, he intercepted a Russell Wilson pass in overtime at the 4-yard line, and the rematch was decided when he stopped Seattle tight end Jacob Hollister right at the goal line on 4th and goal.

And DE Nick Bosa was the consensus defensive rookie of the year, a monster pass rusher and run stopper who motivated his teammates as much as he terrorized opposing quarterbacks.

Going Forward

The 49ers went from having arguably the NFL's least talented roster to one of its most talented, in just three years -- without any infusion of draft picks like the haul that the Rams got in the RGIII trade.

Better yet, John Lynch accomplished it without taking shortcuts, without picking up players after domestic violence incidents, or locking the team into bad contracts or giving away years of draft capital. This roster is young, talented, and has great character.

This masterful rebuild won Lynch the 2019 NFL Executive of the Year award, [47] and it was well deserved.

Rebuilding the Secondary

-- Eric Crocker

As the new league year began in the NFL last March, a common theme among experts and fans were that the 49ers needed to upgrade their biggest weakness, the secondary. From an outside perspective (and fan view) I get it. According to Pro Football Focus, the 49ers secondary was ranked dead last heading into the 2019 season.

Former high school teammates Jimmie Ward and Jaquiski Tartt once again finished the season on the injured reserve list. They had an aging Richard Sherman who was now one year removed from an Achilles injury, and Ahkello Witherspoon heading into his third season after a year two that included an injury and benching. Somehow Witherspoon picked up the pieces and put it together to string together a terrific second half to the 2018 season, only to end with a knee injury that sidelined him the last two regular season games.

The most consistent defender and maybe most underrated player on the defense from a season ago was slot corner K'Waun Williams. Everywhere else there were question marks, including safety Adrian Colbert.

When the free agency period was starting, a lot of people expected the 49ers to go big by adding a cornerback and a safety. I had expressed how the only safety I could have seen the 49ers signing was Earl Thomas, a veteran who was familiar with the scheme, and someone that a young safety such as Adrian Colbert could learn from.

Signing any other safety to a big contract without seeing if Colbert could get back his 2017 mojo seemed counterproductive. You draft players to develop them. Giving up on them after one down season when they have shown signs of being able to play at a high level didn't seem like a route I'd think the 49ers would take. At the bare minimum, you have to give that player an opportunity during training camp.

Instead of paying a high-priced free agent, the 49ers elected to bring back defensive back Jimmie Ward. Ward would be returning to his natural position of safety after being yanked around, playing several different positions over his first five seasons in the NFL. The Niners' fan base wasn't pleased with this signing but Jimmie Ward is a good football player when healthy (the key words being "when healthy").

49ers fans and columnists alike also wanted the 49ers to pay a high-priced free agent cornerback. It was never going to happen. Why not? Well, although Witherspoon had been up and down, there were still ups from the 2017 third rounder. Ideally you'd like to see if he can put together a complete season.

Behind him was another third rounder, Tarvarius Moore, who was drafted in 2018. Moore filled in for Witherspoon briefly at the end of the season but there definitely was not enough film on him to properly assess him moving forward. At least not enough film to pay a high priced free agent to leap frog both Moore and Witherspoon.

How do you address this situation? You want to create competition, so you sign a low priced veteran cornerback to compete with both Moore and Witherspoon. That cornerback was Jason Verrett. The pro bowl corner had played a grand total of five games over the previous three seasons.

Another popular idea was addressing both cornerback and safety in the draft. Both still seemed highly unlikely to me. Like spending money on a prize free agent, a high draft pick at cornerback would mean that player would likely have to play over Witherspoon and Moore. But what if you got the Witherspoon that closed out the season? Or what if your super athletic 2018 third round pick Tarvarius Moore improved with more experience at his new position? Addressing cornerback in the middle rounds made little sense as well.

The same could be said for the safety position. Addressing the free safety position in the draft with Jimmie Ward coming back as insurance and Adrian Colbert showing the ability to play safety at a high level, do you draft a safety in the top three rounds to play over Colbert? You definitely don't draft a safety to compete with Colbert because if he is who you think he is, he beats out that high draft pick and it's now a wasted pick.

Ultimately the 49ers ran into a "wait and see" situation with their young talent with hopes of getting a clearer picture of how to address the secondary after the 2019 season. But what happened next, nobody, including myself could foresee coming.

If I would've told you that the 49ers would have the number one pass defense in the NFL throughout the season, most people would've thought I was crazy. But that's exactly what happened. With an improved pass rush and another year in Robert Saleh's scheme, the 49ers allowed a league-best 169 passing yards per game.

Maybe we should've seen the improvement coming. In Saleh's first season as defensive coordinator of the 49ers they had the 22nd best pass defense. The following 2018 season showed they were headed in the right direction when the 49ers finished the season with the 11th best pass defense, which is even more impressive when you factor in all of the injuries the secondary endured. Which leads us right to 2019.

The total passing yards surrendered were not the only impressive thing about this season. The 49ers defense ranked first in yards per game, yards per attempt and yards per catch. They also allowed the fewest explosive plays on the season.

The story of the 49ers 2019 secondary wasn't written in a straight line. After a tremendous start to the season, Ahkello Witherspoon was sidelined with a foot injury that limited him to eight starts on the year. When he returned to the starting line up his play was up and down.

That wasn't the case for the second year cornerback Emmanuel Moseley who had spent most of his rookie season on the practice squad. Moseley's first career start came in week five of 2019, against the Cleveland Browns on Monday Night Football. After such a hot start to the season by Witherspoon, many doubted if Moseley had the ability to continue 'Spoon's stellar play at the right cornerback position.

Now you are probably thinking, "Moseley? What happened to Tarvarius Moore?" After several training camp injuries to the safety position, Moore was moved back to his college position of safety. So let's go back to Moseley.

I spoke with him prior to the Browns game. He had a solid foundation. A young man who had strong beliefs in himself and the Lord. A self confidence that came from hard work and preparation. So when Moseley got the start and played well, it was a surprise to most, but not him.

Moseley's play was so good that it left most fans asking the question "Does Witherspoon get his spot back?" He did, when he returned from injury, but Witherspoon had a tough stretch of games late in the season. 49ers fans called for Moseley to replace him, and they got their wish.

Moseley replaced Witherspoon late in the crucial week 17 game against the Seahawks, where he made a game saving pass break up on the goal line while guarding rookie DK Metcalf -- who is five inches taller than him, at 6'4".

And then he replaced Witherspoon again in the first quarter of the divisional playoff game against the

Minnesota Vikings, after Ahkello gave up a first quarter touchdown. Minnesota's passing game dried up

The following week against Green Bay Packers, Moseley got the start and again did not disappoint. His first career post-season interception came against the great Aaron Rodgers, a play I'm sure he'll remember for the rest of his life.

The Super Bowl however was a different story. The 49ers cornerbacks were playing a softer coverage to take away the Kansas City Chiefs' deep ball. Moseley was involved in a gut punching play late in the game when the Chiefs converted on a third and 15 play.

The team had rotated into a cover 3, and many people blamed Moseley for not being in his deep third. I'll take a moment now to discuss how cover three works. From a very basic standpoint the field is split up into deep thirds with the left cornerback, middle of the field safety and the right cornerback. The corners have responsibility for the area from to the hash to the sideline. The safety has what's in between that.

All coverages have rules. The good offensive play callers know how to attack coverage rules. So while Moseley has deep third coverage, he also has his reads. In cover three, cornerbacks read "two to one," one being the receiver closest to the sideline in your zone and two being the second closest. If two goes away to where he is no longer a threat in your third or is running into the MOF safety's third, the cornerback can now focus on one if he's still pushing vertical.

On this particular play in the Super Bowl, Emmanuel Moseley had two threats running vertical in his zone, Tyreek Hill and Sammy Watkins. Around 20 yards downfield from the line of scrimmage, Hill started going post, giving Moseley the indication that he can now focus on Watkins, who ran a deep in-breaking route around 20 yards downfield. Ideally you would like your cornerback to squeeze that, shrinking the passing window in a zone.

However, as I alluded to earlier, good play callers know how to attack coverage rules. So once Hill went post towards the MOF safety, Moseley squeezed the deep dig, and Hill came back out, essentially running a deep post corner with plenty of room for Chiefs quarterback Patrick Mahomes to throw into a huge voided area.

Aside from not winning the Super Bowl, 2019 was an amazing season for the 49ers secondary, a group that looks to continue getting better.

John Lynch has a big decision on whether to retain starting safety Jimmie Ward. All-Pro cornerback Richard Sherman isn't getting any younger. If the 49ers were ever going to be aggressive with addressing the cornerback position, this off season would be the time to do it.

Kwon Alexander's LEGENDARY personality

-- Akash Anavarathan

It was 10:47 AM PT on the first day of NFL free agency and my phone buzzed and lit up with a notification from Twitter. Like many football fans, I turn on tweet notifications for *ESPN's* Adam Schefter and *NFL Network's* Ian Rapaport when the open signing period commences. That's the easiest way to keep up given the number of contracts that are handed out in the first few days.

I peered down at the notification and my jaw dropped: the 49ers had signed former Buccaneers' linebacker Kwon Alexander to a four-year, $54 million contract. I thought to myself: "Is this the same player that missed a majority of the 2018 season with a torn ACL?"

San Francisco was in a desperate spot. They had severed ties with former first-round linebacker Reuben Foster who proved that his off-field problems out-weighed his on-field production. The 49ers had a promising young second-year player in middle linebacker Fred Warner, but were missing his running mate at weak-side linebacker (the WILL position).

Think about the dominant defenses in our lifetime and there's usually a pair of linebackers that come to mind. 2013 Seattle had Bobby Wagner and K.J. Wright. 2015 Carolina had Luke Kuechly and Thomas Davis. 2011 San Francisco had Patrick Willis and NaVorro Bowman.

Robert Saleh's defense was 50 percent of the way there with Warner, but they couldn't possibly go into the season with Elijah Lee or Mark Nzeocha lined up next to the former BYU star. That wasn't going to cut it in a league filled with speedy running backs and pass-catching tight ends.

49ers' general manager John Lynch had quite the war chest of spending money to round out a roster that finished 4-12 the previous season. To their credit, San Francisco's brain trust cut their losses with Foster and decided to move in a different direction.

In a free-agent class that was filled with stars from former Raven C.J. Moseley to ex-Eagle Jordan Hicks, the 49ers decided to give $27 million guaranteed to a player coming off of reconstructive knee surgery.

It was 10:47 AM Pacific Time, so San Francisco was aggressive and made the Alexander a priority signing on the opening morning of free agency.

It perplexed me that Lynch and Co. would add a linebacker that was coming off of such a brutal injury in a day and age where quickness and shiftiness in coverage is imperative to playing the position.

Nearly 10 months after the signing, I could not have been more wrong about Alexander and his influence on the rest of the locker room. The former Buccaneer went from being a swing and miss free-agent signing to the heartbeat of this franchise and city.

On the field, the 24-year old worked himself back into game shape before the regular season commenced, which was a surprise given the normal recovery time for an ACL injury. At his introductory press conference, Alexander could not contain his excitement to get back out there, adding "I can't wait. I'm itching right now."

Alexander was the missing piece to Saleh's defensive puzzle, as his on-the-field dominance and off-the-field leadership was exactly what needed to elevate this unit from good to outstanding.

Yet on Halloween, the injury gods played a mean trick on the 49ers' WILL linebacker as Alexander suffered a torn pectoral injury and was placed on injured reserve. It's an injury that would take a normal human six months to recover, putting Alexander's hopes of returning to the field in the 2019 season to rest.

"Legendary."

That's what the ex-LSU linebacker kept saying to reporters as he was attempting to return from this injury in miraculous fashion. 49ers' wide receiver Kendrick Bourne kept posting pictures on Instagram that showed Alexander's work on the practice field, but some part of me kept not wanting to believe that he would possibly return this season.

At the same time, Texans' star defensive end J.J. Watt was recovering from the same injury on roughly the same timeline. 49ers' fans paid close attention to Watt's eventual return because it increased hope that Alexander could return to the 49ers' defense.

San Francisco's defense was among the best in the NFL when Alexander manned the middle of the field and they regressed when he missed time due to the pectoral injury, giving up 46 points to the Saints, 29 to the Falcons and 31 to the Rams in back-to-back-to-back weeks.

49ers' head coach Kyle Shanahan was cautiously optimistic when speaking on Alexander's potential return to the team, constantly downplaying his chances of a post-season return.

That all changed after San Francisco clinched the No. 1 seed in the NFC, and announced that they would be activating Kwon Alexander from injured reserve status. He would make his playoff debut against the Vikings when the 49ers began their postseason run.

Every defensive player was outwardly gushing about the Alexander's re-entry to the team, because it meant more than just the tackles and sacks he put on the stat sheet. Alexander's brightly-dyed red hair, combined with his infectious smile and constant positivity represented everything that the 2019 49ers' team stood for.

Shanahan and Lynch have embraced a culture that allowed players to outwardly display their true personality and it created an organic locker room that Alexander embodied in his daily actions.

The 49ers' head coach always believed that if his team's players can be themselves daily, then that will allow to play their best football on the field. Nobody carries that attitude with them better than Alexander.

San Francisco's linebacker crew had donned the phrase "Hot Boyzzz" and "The block is hot" all season long and it began to resonate with the rest of the locker room and fans. Other players started to wear sweatshirts with these slogans before games and fans quickly joined in.

Kwon's return to the field was electrifying, providing a much-needed boost to a 49ers' defense that limped to the regular season finish line. His play, combined with a healthy Dee Ford and Jaquiski Tartt allowed the 49ers to limit their two high-scoring NFC playoff opponents to a combined 30 points.

Alexander isn't just a starting middle linebacker for the 49ers, he's the backbone of this team's identity. I couldn't have imagined writing those words when he signed in the offseason, but with the rest and recovery that Alexander will get this offseason, he's bound to get better and better.

Dre Greenlaw
-- Kyle Breitkreutz

When the 49ers drafted Dre Greenlaw, fans didn't know much about him. He was a safety in high school and a four-year starter at outside linebacker for Arkansas, facing SEC competition But he missed 8 of 48 college games with a broken foot his sophomore year and a high ankle sprain as a senior, then skipped several tests (40-yard dash, 3-cone, and 20- and 60-yard shuttles) at the combine.

Critics were quick to point out his lack of size (at 5'11", 237), and Lance Zeirlein of NFL.com saw

> *"a lack of willful aggression to fire downhill and put his stamp on games... nothing more than clean-up tackles on his own side of the ball."* [48]

Hilariously, Zeirlein quoted an anonymous "NFL area scout" as saying

> *"I don't think he's tough enough to trust him in a game. He better be really good on special teams unless he finds more dog inside him."*

The 49ers front office was not swayed and took him in the 5th round of the 2019 draft, perhaps noticing that he was highly productive in the 40 games he did play. In his first year, Greenlaw had led all SEC freshman with 95 tackles. His 9 games as a senior generated 80 tackles, 6.5 TFL, 2 sacks and 2 interceptions.

John Lynch, aided by Adam Peters and the rest of the front office personnel staff, have hit on several fifth round prospects during their tenure with the 49ers. Trent Taylor and George Kittle in the 2017 class, D.J. Reed in the 2018 class, and now Dre Greenlaw. Fittingly named "Big Play Dre", Greenlaw was known for his speed and playmaking ability in college; he always seemed around the football.

When Lynch took over as general manager, he had promised the Faithful that he would build a team with the right kind of people, both on and off the field. Greenlaw was no exception. Just a few minutes after Dre was drafted, a story popped up on Twitter from Gerry Dales, the father of a student who attended college with him. [49]

> *"My daughter went to a college party when she was a freshman. She knew very few people, and didn't have a ton of experience drinking. Someone slipped something into her drink when she wasn't paying attention.*
>
> *Greenlaw was from Fayetteville and knew her from high school, but didn't know the guy who was giving her attention. When that guy tried to steer her out the door, [Greenlaw] stopped the guy and said, 'She's not going anywhere.'"*

At this time, Greenlaw was a starter for the Razorbacks, and as Mr. Dales pointed out:

> *"His place was not secure. He was underage and at a 'kegger'. He wasn't drinking, but if there was a fight, he was risking getting thrown off the team. In some ways risking 'everything' to protect her."*

After the party, Dales' daughter went to the hospital to get her stomach pumped, to remove the drug that she had been dosed with. The next day, she called Greenlaw to thank him. During a media session with reporters in the 49ers rookie minicamp, Dre acknowledged the story and said he was "Just looking out for a friend."

One thing was certain: the 49ers front office had drafted a young player with the ability to come in day-one and compete, as well as a guy that fans would want to cheer for. This was only 153 days after the team had released former first-round pick Reuben Foster following a domestic battery arrest. It was clear that John Lynch had decided to stay true to his promise, and he got an exciting football player and a great person in Dre Greenlaw as a result.

Azeez Al-Shaair's camp battle
-- Kyle Breitkreutz

Azeez Al-Shaair was an undrafted free agent (UDFA) coming out of Florida Atlantic University. The odds are stacked against success even for drafted players, and UDFAs face a particularly rough road.
There are only 1,696 roster slots in the entire NFL, including all of the veterans, and more than 224 college players are drafted each year.

Linebackers Fred Warner, Kwon Alexander and rookie Dre Greenlaw were locks to make the team at linebacker, leaving two slots to fill at the position. There were five other players competing with Al-Shaair for one of these positions: three returning 49ers veterans (Elijah Lee, Mark Nzeocha, and Malcolm Smith) and two other newcomers. They were:
-- LaRoy Reynolds, a "special teams ace" in Atlanta, and
-- David Mayo, a player with some starting experience in Carolina, but also primarily a special teamer.

However, Al-Shaair was no stranger to adversity, to overcoming the odds in order to push through. Talking to Matt Maiocco on *The 49ers Insider Podcast*, he compared his life story to a novel.

> *"You turn through the pages of the book and at first it's like, 'I really don't like this book.' Then, you keep reading and keep reading, and, 'You know what? This turned out pretty good.' That's kind of an accumulation of how my life has been."* [50]

When Azeez was young, his parents divorced, and he, his mother and seven siblings ended up staying at his grandmother's house. Then in 2012 that house burned down, leaving them homeless. There were days where he didn't know when his next meal would be or where he would sleep, but he fought through it all and found his way to the NFL.

After all of that, finding a roster spot seemed like absolutely nothing.

His first opportunity to show what he could do came in a preseason game against the Dallas Cowboys on August 10th. He was given 34 snaps to show the coaching staff and front office what he could do, the 3rd most among linebackers during the game, and he finished with 4 tackles, one fumble recovery and one tackle for a loss.

The one tackle for loss was notable and possibly the most significant for roster spot implications. The Cowboys were looking to put away the game, clinging to a 9-7 lead. Faced with a 3rd & 10 on Dallas' 43 yard line, they came out in a four WR set, with Azeez the only linebacker on the field. Quarterback Mike White faked a handoff to Mike Weber, but Al-Shaair correctly diagnosed it as a screen pass to Weber. He exploded into the backfield to light up Weber for a five-yard loss.

The play fired up the entire 49ers team. Kwon Alexander and Fred Warner immediately went to Azeez to celebrate the huge hit with him, followed by the rest of the defense. The 49ers scored a touchdown on the following drive and won, 17-9.

As the preseason went on, the players made the 49ers' decision difficult. The first domino dropped following the 49ers 3rd preseason game versus the Chiefs, the game where players the team plans on keeping play the most. Malcolm Smith, an expensive free agent who was considered a bust, was cut in favor of WR Nick Williams.

All that remained was the fourth preseason game, the one where keepers play the least. Surprisingly, the 49ers coaching staff didn't give Al-Shaair much of an opportunity to play; he finished the game with only one tackle.

On paper, he was outplayed by David Mayo, LaRoy Reynolds, and Elijah Lee, who was once considered likely to start alongside Fred Warner and Kwon Alexander.

But in the backwards logic of preseason football, not playing much in game four was a good sign. The coaches already liked what they saw from the rookie, and didn't need to see any more.

On August 31st 2019, Azeez's dream came true. The 49ers decided to move on from Mayo, Reynolds and Lee while keeping Nzeocha and Al-Shaair along with Greenlaw, Alexander and Warner. He was a 49er.

Chapter 4. September

at Tampa Bay Buccaneers, September 8th, 2019
49ers win, 31-17

at Cincinnati Bengals, September 15th, 2019
49ers win, 41-17

vs. Pittsburgh Steelers, September 22nd, 2019
49ers win, 24-20

Bye week, September 29th, 2019

The 2019 San Francisco 49ers were doubted, mocked and dismissed all year, from the first day of OTAs (organized team activities) in April right up through the Super Bowl (where they were 1.5 point underdogs).

Even though quarterback Jimmy Garoppolo would be back from injury on a team that everyone could see was improving, there was something about this team -- perhaps the lack of stars and divas -- that consistently made people underestimate them.

One of the worst takes came over the summer from the NFL Network's self-appointed "irreverent" analyst, Adam Rank. He forecast the team to go 3-13, beating only the Bengals, Browns, and Cardinals (and Arizona only one out of two games).

On Twitter, the website 49ers Hub asked people what they thought of this prediction,[51] but we can't print most of the (admittedly incisive) responses. (See separate article.)

Another reason was the beginning of a bad year of injuries. Most notably, Jerick (Jet) McKinnon was lost for the second straight season after an unspecified setback (reportedly not on his same right knee) required another surgery. At this point, he'll need to be superb in 2020 training camp to ever play for the 49ers. His guaranteed money has all been paid, and his base salary jumps up to $6.5 million dollars in 2020.

Slot receiver Trent Taylor, who had been Jimmy Garoppolo's favorite receiver before back injuries knocked him out, was having a great training camp before he suffered a "Jones fracture" (a stress fracture of the fifth metatarsal bone in his foot) [52] that required surgery in early August.

Doctors put a screw in his foot to speed healing, but that screw caused irritation, requiring a second surgery; then his foot got infected, ending Taylor's season. [53] He had his fifth surgery on January 2, 2020 and hopes to be back for OTAs in the spring. [54]

Newly-acquired pass rusher Dee Ford developed tendinitis in his knee and missed a week of practice after receiving platelet-rich plasma treatment on his knee at the beginning of August.

Star rookie Nick Bosa fought through some injury problems as well. His college career was cut short by a bilateral core muscle injury that caused him to withdraw from Ohio State, missing most of his senior season to recover from surgery and prepare for the draft.

In OTAs, he suffered a hamstring sprain that caused him to miss three weeks. Then in training camp, Bosa rolled his right ankle badly enough to require a walking boot. He missed the entire preseason and was literally limping into the regular season.

Then rookie wide receiver Jalen Hurd -- also performing well in the preseason -- hurt his back in a joint practice with Denver. It was described as "stiffness" at first but when the team called him "week to week" before the first game, it was clearly something worse.

By late September, the team was calling it a stress fracture and when they put him on injured reserve list on October 3rd, it sounded more like a broken back. Shanahan kept holding out the possibility that the rookie might return later in the season, but later reported multiple "setbacks." Hurd never played a snap.

To top it all off, safety Jimmie Ward broke a finger at the end of the preseason, requiring surgery to repair it. He didn't play until week 5 in Cleveland.

Game 1: Tampa Bay Buccaneers

Expectations were not high for the season's first game. Jimmy Garoppolo hadn't played a regular season game in nearly a year, and the Niners were coming off of a 4-12 season, down several players.

Meanwhile, Tampa Bay had brought in impressive new talent at coach (Bruce Arians) and defensive coordinator (Todd Bowles), aiming to fix a terrible secondary and make the most of their offensive talent (quarterback Jameis Winston and receivers Mike Evans and Chris Godwin).

The betting line ranged from even to Tampa Bay by a point. Since the game was in Tampa, that signals a small advantage for San Francisco, less the standard 3-point home field advantage.

This was an ugly game, even if you like defensive slugfests. Four fumbles, four interceptions, and four touchdowns called back on penalties (two for each team). Kwon Alexander, who played for Tampa Bay in 2018, was ejected in the first quarter after a late him on Winston.

21 of the 48 total points came on pick-sixes, and Jimmy Garoppolo blew a lot of yards-after-catch opportunities with inaccurate but completed passes. For those quick slants to really hit, he needs to hit his receivers in stride.

The first half ended 7-6 Tampa; San Francisco had only gained 131 yards, but they held the Bucs to 100. It never got much prettier than that. There were 19 penalties for 174 yards combined, and lots of great field position (by both teams) that resulted in a field goal or no points at all.

Tampa Bay ended two drives inside the San Francisco ten-yard line, fumbling it away once and getting stopped on

4th-and-2. San Francisco lost a fumble at Tampa Bay's 23-yard line right before halftime.

In the end, though, the Niners came away with a 31-17 win. Garoppolo's 39-yard touchdown pass to Richie James, Jr. was the prettiest play of the day, but pick-sixes by Richard Sherman and Ahkello Witherspoon decided the game. Tarvarius Moore also played well in Ward's place.

It was not an especially encouraging game for Niners fans -- until they saw Tampa Bay play Carolina 4 days later on Thursday night.

In week one, the Los Angeles Rams -- in their first game after the Super Bowl -- had barely hung on against a strong Carolina team, 30 - 27, as Christian McCaffrey totaled more receiving yards AND more rushing yards than anyone on the defending NFC champions.

Four days later, it became clear how much Todd Bowles had improved Tampa Bay's defense. The Buccaneers thumped that same Carolina team 20-14, winning on a 4th quarter goal line stand. Christian McCaffrey got only 16 yards on 6 pass targets, and 37 yards on 16 carries.

Meanwhile, Jameis Winston looked great, 16 of 25 for 208 yards, a touchdown and a passer rating of 103.4, while Chris Godwin and Mike Evans averaged over 15 yards per reception. Tampa Bay looked pretty darned good when they weren't playing San Francisco.

It was hard to know at the time, but in hindsight, two key strengths of this 49ers team emerged. And both of them were connected to new assistant coaches.

First, the secondary was drastically improved under new Defensive Passing Game coordinator Joe Woods. Even if you ignored the defensive touchdowns, those three interceptions were more than San Francisco produced in all 16 games of 2018, when they set the all-time NFL record for fewest INTs, with 2.

Second, that secondary and Kris Kocurek's revamped defensive line had learned how to stuff short-yardage situations. All year long, 3rd and 1 or 2, and 4th & 1 or 2, were advantage Niners. In this case, Tarvarius Moore broke up a pass to Chris Godwin on 4th-and-2.

Bruce Arians is known for his "No Risk It, No Biscuit" philosophy, and you can see that he's enjoyed a lot of biscuits over the years. But in week one, the 49ers left him hungry.

Week 2: Cincinnati Bengals

Cincinnati had a lot of hype too, between new coach Zac Taylor and a near upset of the Seahawks in Seattle. (They lost 21-20.) The Vegas line was a point and a half in favor of the Bengals.

Instead, San Francisco demolished them 41-17, dominating in every aspect of the game including 572 yards of total offense. Kwon Alexander intercepted another pass, and Matt Breida ran for 121 yards -- which was less than half of the team's massive rushing total. He did average over 10 yards a carry, though.

The team had decided to spend the week in Youngstown, Ohio between weeks one and two, instead of flying home and crossing 5 more time zones. Coach Shanahan is a big believer in matching game conditions ahead of time, practicing them in every way possible. In the week before the Super Bowl, he even had the team practice the extra long halftime just so they would be used to it.

Jimmy Garoppolo was a fan of the stay over, after he'd thrown three touchdowns and completed 17 of 25 passes for 259 yards. He told reporters that

> *"The week in Youngstown definitely paid off. There was extra time to be around each other and talk about things."*

(What he probably meant by that was that he wasn't distracted by the temptation to date porn stars.)

Kyle Shanahan showed off his clever play calling, as Garoppolo lateralled to WR Dante Pettis -- who threw a 16-yard pass to RB Raheem Mostert. And the coach got a chance to run his favorite play -- the "leak" -- on the first offensive drive, with a brand new player.

The leak is a play-action pass where a blocker (typically TE Kittle or FB Juszczyk) lines up next to a tackle to block the outside zone run and jogs along with the offensive linemen for a few seconds while Garoppolo runs a bootleg. Maybe the target even blocks somebody. Then he ever-so-casually slips downfield on a sort of delayed wheel route and goes deep.

The twist this time was that the target was Marquise Goodwin, demonstrating how Shanahan fools defenses by running the same concept with different skill players. Goodwin lined up on the right side of the offensive line, a bit smaller than his neighbors at 5'9, 181, but who expects a receiver in that spot anyway? No one was examining him too closely after he started blocking, least of all the linebacker responsible for him in pass coverage.

Goodwin leaked downfield and could not have been more wide open. 38 yards, touchdown San Francisco.

The injuries continued, however. Nick Bosa, still hobbled by his ankle sprain, had played just 38 snaps against Tampa Bay, and that dropped to 31 plays against Cincinnati, but he looked much better. On the other hand, Dee Ford missed the second half after aggravating his knee and adding a quadriceps injury. He would injured on and off all year.

Worst of all, left tackle Joe Staley broke his leg (fibula). He would be out for many weeks, though not the whole season. This was an even bigger problem because the backup swing tackle, Shon Coleman, had been lost for the season in training camp. The only reserve tackles left were 6th round pick Justin Skule, and undrafted free agent Daniel Brunskill.

Some teams would have picked up another tackle, but there just weren't any good ones on the market except Washington's Trent Williams -- and their front office reportedly refused to deal with a Shanahan team, due to bad blood left over from the end of his offensive coordinator stint there.

So Skule went in, and Shanahan altered his play-calling to protect his quarterback's blind side. Staley went out with 2:26 left in the third, and Shanahan only called one pass after that -- out of 21 plays.

Despite Staley's injury, the team was very excited. The game plan, the schemes, the new players -- it was all coming together just the way that Shanahan had told them. And the wider football world was noticing, too.

The Sporting News' power rankings put San Francisco -- the second worst team in the league in 2018 -- at #8 after two games. To give you an idea how powerful the NFC West is, though, they were still ranked third in their division, behind Seattle (#7) and the Los Angeles Rams (#4). It would take a lot more than two wins to change the power balance in the division.

Richard Sherman, the wily veteran who had played on Seattle's Super Bowl teams, urged caution and continued focus amid all the celebration. He knew the stakes were a lot higher than one or two big victories on the road.

> *"This is a franchise that won five championships, and we're trying to get back to that. It's a work in progress."*

Week 3: Pittsburgh Steelers

Just like the Bengals, Pittsburgh came into this game having played the Seahawks close, losing just 28-26. However there was a reason they were predicted to lose to San Francisco by a touchdown. Against Seattle, QB Ben Roethlisberger only lasted one half, and had elbow surgery that ended his season a day after the game.

San Francisco would face the mighty Mason Rudolph, who had looked pretty solid in relief against Seattle (passer rating of 92.4), but still.... The Vegas line was just under a touchdown, at 6.5 points, though most sportswriters had it closer: San Francisco by 3 or 4. [55]

The sportswriters were right. This game was even uglier than week one, as the Niners turned it over FIVE TIMES, but still managed to grind out a 24-20 victory when Garoppolo hit Dante Pettis for a five-yard touchdown with just 1:15 left in the game.

The Niners fumbled snaps twice inside the Pittsburgh ten-yard line; one shotgun snap hit Richie James as he came by in motion, and Garoppolo couldn't corral a too-short hike from center Weston Richburg.

The QB was 23 for 32 (277 yards) to ten different receivers, though, and it was hard to blame him for two first half interceptions that went off his receivers' hands. K'Waun Williams intercepted Rudolph, as well.

The best play of the game came on a pass up the middle to Kyle Juszczyk. Juice lined up in the slot at the San Francisco 38 yard line, "let a blocker dodge him" and went straight out, uncovered.

Star cornerback Minkah Fitzpatrick, who the Steelers had just acquired tried to clean it up by tackling the fullback coming in from his right side.

Juszczyk put up a cocked left arm and threw Fitzpatrick to the ground across his body, like an annoying little brother who had just jumped off the couch onto him, then stomped ahead through another tackler for ten more yards. The play was of course on every highlight reel that day.

Juszczyk, second only to Kittle in receiving with 53 yards on three targets, also caught a 27-yard bomb on a go route with a beautiful diving catch.

Afterwards, the pundits all gravely intoned that it's always going to be difficult to win when you turn the ball over five times. DUH. The amazing thing is the Niners were good enough to turn it over five times and win anyway.

Meanwhile, the Niners had made gains that weren't being noticed. In their first three games -- two of them on the road -- they only had a single 3-and-out.

Week 4: Bye

For most teams, week four is way earlier than they want for their bye. The first possible bye week, it leaves you with 13 straight games, some on short weeks, to end the season.

For this Niners team though, the injuries were so thick that the team was happy to take any break it could get. The extra time enabled Nick Bosa to get fully healthy for the first time. Even limited, he had notched 17 pressures in 3 games. But he only had one sack so far, and his ambitions were much greater than that.

The team hoped that the extra time would help them heal up CB Jason Verrett and WR Jalen Hurd, and it definitely let Staley cut the number of games he'd miss by one.

The Adam Rank 3-13 prediction

-- Kyle Breitkreutz

Entering the season, there were some analysts who were high on the 49ers, but there were more who weren't too positive regarding the direction of the franchise. They were coming off a 4-12 season, and had a QB returning from a devastating knee injury, questions regarding the wide receivers and defensive backs, and just a lot of overall skepticism.

One analyst stood out from the rest: the *NFL Network's* own Adam Rank. On his "State of the Franchise" segment, Rank covered all 32 teams and gave a preview of how he feels each team will do that year.

49ers HUB
@49ersHub

Please, please respond to this in the form of GIFs

6:49 AM · Jun 18, 2019 · Twitter for iPhone

In the 49ers segment, he went in on the team and how tough their schedule was, repeating "That's a loss. That's a loss." It seemed like each game he previewed was going to be tough (if not impossible) for the 49ers to win.

By the time he totaled up all of the games, he had forecast a 3-13 record -- actually worse than their 2018 record, which had earned them the second highest draft pick (Nick Bosa).

This sent 49ers fans into an absolute frenzy. All over social media, The Faithfull were sharing pictures, sharing the video, challenging him on his analysis.

Rank then doubled down on his analysis in an August article at NFL.com titled, "Unpopular Opinions: 49ers overhyped; Bills deserve more love." [56]

In the very first line, Adam admits that "I don't get the 49ers." He could not have imagined how prophetic this statement would prove to be.

He noted that Jimmy Garoppolo hadn't started more than seven games in any NFL season, and that his 2018 before the ACL injury had been looking like a disaster. The 49ers' talent was "not terrible, just fine", he thought, but they had zero pass catchers outside of George Kittle. Their defense was ranked 28th (out of 32) in scoring in 2018, and had the fewest takeaways in NFL history.

All of which were fair criticisms at the time -- but only if you think the team had done nothing to improve over the off-season and was not on a path toward improvement.

However fair or unfair his criticisms seemed to be, it was the combination of these two analyses that would become a season long focus for 49ers fans when watching the 49ers play.

Richard Sherman had the perfect answer:

> *"You want idiots to sound like idiots but you want them to hold their position the whole year. Like don't flip-flop with us. If you said we weren't going to make it, if you said we were some way early on, stick with that position. Hold it.*
>   *Don't try to give us credit now, just stick. If you had us ranked 25, keep us ranked 25. If you had us going home early, if you had us going three-and-whatever, have us going three-and-whatever. You know what I mean? At least stick by your word because I want you sounding like an idiot at the end."* [57]

Chapter 5. October

vs. Cleveland Browns, Monday October 7th, 2019
49ers win, 31-3

at Los Angeles Rams, October 13th, 2019
49ers win, 20-7

at Washington, October 20th, 2019
49ers win, 9-0

vs. Carolina Panthers, October 27th, 2019
49ers win, 51-13

at Arizona Cardinals Thursday October 31st, 2019
49ers win, 28-25

October started with optimism and concern. The optimism flowed naturally after three wins against East Coast teams, two on the road.

But so did the concerns, which were based on injuries and a disturbing tendency for Jimmy Garoppolo to throw stupid interceptions, often to linebackers right in front of him that he seemed unable to see.

It was like a unique variant of color-blindedness, and if it hadn't cost the team any games yet, no one expected that luck to continue.

Week 5. Cleveland Browns

Coming out of the bye, San Francisco was rested and somewhat healed. First up was Cleveland, another team that felt excited and on the verge of a big turnaround. Stinking for so long, they had accumulated a lot of talent with top draft picks, including mobile quarterback Baker Mayfield, and fans were hoping that new coach Freddie Kitchens would unlock their potential -- even if his name sounded like a character in a Martin Scorsese mob movie.

Before the season, Cleveland was picked to make the playoffs by many pundits, while few saw San Francisco getting past both the Rams and Seahawks. An outside chance at a wild card berth was the general consensus.

While Cleveland had lost to the Rams by a touchdown, 20-13 -- impressive in itself given how terrible the Browns have been since, oh, Y2K -- they came right back and stomped the Baltimore Ravens, 40-25. And while this game was in San Francisco, it was set to feature rookie Justin Skule at left tackle, matched up against edge rusher Myles Garrett. That's not good.

The home team was actually favored in Vegas, but no one foresaw what happened - a 31-3 annihilation by the Niners.

Where to start? Oh, how about the first play from scrimmage: Matt Breida for 83 yards, untouched.

Touchdown. He actually waved to Cleveland safety Damarious Randall as he zoomed past him.

Ted Nguyen pointed out in the Athletic that this was stage two of Kyle Shanahan's play-calling. Now that he had established the power of the team's outside zone runs, he could punish teams that tried to stop it with constraint plays:

> *"Additionally, the 49ers offense has several answers for defenses that flow too aggressively to their outside zones like F-counters or outside zone with a fullback wind back like in [the Breida touchdown against Cleveland]."* [58]

On the very next play from scrimmage, Richard Sherman intercepted Baker Mayfield at midfield and ran it back to the Cleveland 41. After a couple of punts and a 49ers touchdown, it was 14-0 (still in the first quarter) and Mayfield was strip-sacked by Bosa, losing the ball.

Later, with 4:45 still left in the first half, Mayfield was intercepted again two yards short of the Niners' end zone by K'Waun Williams, who ran it back to midfield.

It was the worst game of Mayfield's career, breaking a streak of 17 straight games where he threw a touchdown -- every NFL game he'd ever played, in fact. Until October 7th.

Mayfield was 8-22 for only 100 yards, with 4 sacks and 2 interceptions -- a passer rating of 13.4. To top it off, Nick

Bosa "planted the flag" on Mayfield after a sack. (See separate article.)

Matt Breida and Tevin Coleman accounted for 211 of San Francisco's 275 yards rushing.

San Francisco's only real failure in the game was Robbie Gould's kicking, but that was horrible: two missed field goals, and a third one blocked. Given that he held out and forced the 49ers to franchise tag him, this was deeply embarrassing for GM John Lynch.

There's nothing wrong with putting resources into special teams, a high-impact area that many teams neglect (and that serves as a potential springboard for underappreciated players like Raheem Mostert). But when you do, the investment had better pay off.

The Niners had made Gould the highest-paid kicker in the NFL: they ended up signing him for 4 years, $19 million dollars, $10.5 million of which was guaranteed. It was starting to look like they paid top dollar for one of the worst kickers in football, and they were stuck with him for at least two years.

Injuries for all of the blockers

Injury woes continued as well. This win cost San Francisco the services of their two best remaining blockers (aside from TE George Kittle): right tackle Mike McGlinchey -- out 4 to 6 weeks with a knee injury that required arthroscopic surgery -- and fullback Kyle Juszczyk, who left the game with a sprained left knee during the third quarter.

There's no need to explain how devastating it is to lose both of your starting offensive tackles, particularly with the top reserve tackle (Shon Coleman) already out for the year.

But don't overlook the importance of Juszczyk to the running game, either. The Harvard grad is a legitimate passing threat, as Pittsburgh learned, but he's invaluable in the run game -- helping spring Breida on his opening snap touchdown in this game, for example.

The Niners were now undefeated but facing several weeks at least without four of their best five blockers. The starting tackles for the next month or two would be a rookie 6th round pick (Justin Skule) and an undrafted former defensive lineman who was best known (if at all) for his work in the AAF, a football minor league that lasted all of two months.

This is where the multiplicity of Shanahan's scheme, and John Lynch's penchant for versatile players paid off. Every skill player on the Niners is pushed to block, and receivers such as Deebo Samuel, Kendrick Bourne and newly signed 6'3" slot receiver Jordan Matthews were able to chip in, so to speak.

Backup tight ends Ross Dwelley and Levine Toilolo are nowhere near George Kittle as receivers, but they can help push people around -- at least Toilolo can. Shanahan even used defensive tackle Sheldon Day as a blocker in goal line situations. Whatever gets you through the game.

Serving Notice

Injuries and kicking woes aside, this was a night for celebration. The game was on Monday Night Football, with its undivided, national, prime time audience, and now everyone in the U.S. was on notice that this team was for real. San Francisco and New England were the only undefeated teams in the NFL, after just five weeks. It was San Francisco's first 4-0 start since 1990, a team that boasted Joe Montana and Jerry Rice.

Four games, four teams that had started the season hopefully -- until they played the Niners. They all left their matchup dismayed, and were never really the same afterwards.

It was starting to look like San Francisco was not only beating teams, but destroying their confidence in the process. One mark of their domination: San Francisco had not allowed a single rushing touchdown in four games. And their pass defense was better than the run D.

It's not that doubters and haters had disappeared, before or after this game. Witless cries of "But who have they played?" continued right up through the Super Bowl. Those same people didn't doubt the Patriots, handed a cupcake schedule in their weakling division pretty much every year of their 18-year march of greatness. New England played Miami twice in 2019, for heaven's sake.

But after an utterly one-sided destruction of one of the most-hyped NFL teams, Richard Sherman had some measured words for San Francisco skeptics. In fact, he encouraged them to stick to their guns -- and keep being idiots, instead of correcting himself. (See separate article.)

Did he mean the NFL Network's Adam Rank, the guy who had predicted a 3-13 season for San Francisco? Adam Rank certainly thought so. Defying Sherman's challenge, he put out a video on YouTube titled "I AM AN IDIOT ... SORRY 49ERS FANS." [59] I didn't watch it, because I can't stand video of people just talking directly to the camera. But I'm pretty sure he did not stick to his guns.

But the Rank One was not the only doubter that Sherman was referring to, and San Francisco was in fact facing a tougher opponent the following week: division rival and defending NFC champs, the Rams.

Week 6: Los Angeles Rams

It was ironic that people dismissed the Niners' strength because of their schedule, given that in 2019, the NFC West was clearly the toughest division in football. Surging San Francisco was widely ranked behind the Seattle Seahawks, because Russell Wilson, and the Rams, who had just been to the Super Bowl after all.

Then again, the Rams had been humiliated in that game, scoring the fewest points (3) in Super Bowl history, as

Belichick proved that Vic Fangio's method for baffling Goff was replicable.

Just shift your defensive alignment after the coach's microphone is cut off, and make the gritless quarterback read the formation and decide how to respond on his own. Add a 6-1 defensive front to "choke out" the Rams' wide zone runs and make their motion trickery meaningless, [60] and they don't really have a plan B.

Meanwhile Todd Gurley looked shot, hobbled by arthritis in his knee to the point where he was a bog-standard running back at best, and arthritis is not curable, no matter how many copper bracelets you wear.

Both Goff and Gurley were welded to the team for years with expensive, guaranteed contracts. On top of that, the team had let their offensive line deteriorate in the off season (to pinch a few pennies), which predictably made their two big stars even less effective.

By the time San Francisco headed south for the showdown we all knew was coming, the confidence of Rams fans was as brittle as Goff's self-confidence. Through five weeks of the season, there was evidence for both optimists and pessimists about the Rams.

They won their first three games, including an impressive 27-9 win against New Orleans, but when the 49ers entered LA Memorial Coliseum (with thousands of fans who often drowned out the jaded locals), Los Angeles was on a two-game losing streak. Their one-point loss to Seattle on the road was understandable, but giving up 55 points to Tampa Bay at home was concerning.

On the other hand, they had scored 40 points themselves against the Buccaneer's tough defense, and averaged 456 yards per game in those two losses, so maybe the Fangio/Belichick blueprint wasn't a cheat code to stop LA's offense after all. (Seattle had used the 6-1 front in their narrow win.)

Sure enough, LA scored on their first drive against San Francisco without throwing a single pass -- 7 straight runs, 65 yards, 7 points. Gurley wasn't even playing in the game. Clearly they were trying to send a message that San Francisco wasn't going to bully them in this game.

Unfortunately for LA, that just pissed the 49ers off, and they bullied the Rams for the rest of the game. San Francisco held Goff to a career-low 78 yards on 24 attempts-- the first of many quality QBs who had season lows or career lows against San Francisco in 2019 -- and limited LA's total offense to 157 yards.

Los Angeles never scored again after that first drive, while San Francisco notched 8 tackles for loss, 4 sacks for 30 yards lost, and 2 Goff fumbles.

But those raw numbers actually underestimate the Niners' defensive dominance. Look at key plays -- 3rd and 4th downs. Los Angeles did not convert a single one in the entire game. Zero for nine on third down. Zero for four on fourth down. There is not a better way to humiliate an offense.

San Francisco made their reply to the Rams' message about physicality most emphatically with 3:59 left in the first half. LA had a 3rd and goal at the San Francisco one-yard line. They ran it twice. And got stuffed twice.

That was the precise moment that control of the NFC West shifted back to Northern California. After the game, Garoppolo said this about those short-yardage stuffs:

> *"It sparks everybody. Coaches, players, everybody is hollering on the sideline."*

San Francisco ended four of LA's drives by stopping fourth-down attempts, two consecutive drives in the second quarter and two more in the fourth. That's how you send a message about who's going to bully who.

Every time San Francisco took over possession on downs, TV cameras showed the bald-headed Saleh joy-raging and fist pumping on the sideline, sparking Twitter jokes about steroids and Red Bull.

He told reporters after the game that:

> *"I'm not going to lie. I black out during those moments. I get excited for the guys and their success. When they make big plays, I feel like I'm right there with them. When we fail, I'm right there with them, too. So, we're always together."*

The interesting thing is that San Francisco did *not* follow the Fangio/Belichick blueprint in shutting down the Rams.

Here is Saleh's description of how they reacted to LA's opening drive touchdown:

> *"There was absolutely no panic. We didn't need to change our calls. We didn't need to change the structure of the defense. We felt good going into this game with our front, just our front, without having to do anything like that 6-1 [front that] other teams have been doing."*

They did, however, make another key adjustment described by Ted Nguyen in The Athletic: they slanted their defensive front a step to the weak side (the side of the line that the tight end is *not* on).

> *"This strategy was effective because it made it much harder to run outside zone to the weak side, which McVay likes to do, and made it hard for the Rams to double-team their defensive linemen when they ran to the strong side.*
> *It essentially forced the Rams running backs to bounce outside on strong-side runs and Saleh was confident that the 49ers' team speed and secondary tackling were good enough to stop outside runs."* [61]

In other words, Saleh (and DL coach Kris Kocurek) decided to take away the counter-intuitive run to the weak side (where you have one fewer blocker, but the distance to daylight is shorter), and dare the Rams to try to run it wide on the strong side. They were betting they would win a footrace to the edge, and they were right.

Week 7: Washington

This game was dull and ugly, as a bad team (at home) fought a good team crippled by injuries and slowed by monsoon rains and mid-field lakes. The score was 0-0 at halftime, and Robbie Gould -- in a comeback from his erratic early season play -- scored every point of the game on three field goals for a 9-0 win. (He did miss a 45-yarder in the first half, though.)

Marquise Goodwin left the game after being tested for a concussion.

It was a revenge game for Kyle Shanahan, fired as Washington's offensive coordinator in 2013, and every win is a good thing, but it wasn't much of a showcase for his offensive cleverness. Richard Sherman called it the "Mud Bowl."

> *"It takes you back to being a kid: You're out there, you're sloshing around and your shoes are full of water and mud. It's still a kid's game at the end of the day. Guys had a lot of fun slipping and sliding out there, but winning's always fun."*

Sherman was referring to the highlight of the game, which came when it ended. Not just the fact that it ended, though that was wonderful too. Nick Bosa sacked Case Keenum to squelch the last second comeback attempt, then dove onto the field like it was a football player-sized slip-and-slide. Bosa skidded for miles (about 20 yards, to be precise) and several of his teammates joined him in an exuberant, joyful end to a few hours of misery.

But slice it any way you want, San Francisco remained undefeated in game conditions that undercut all of their strategic advantages.

New England and the Niners take each other's measure

After seven weeks of play, SF and New England were the only undefeated teams left in football. They were also the two dominant defenses in the NFL.

The conventional wisdom is that Bill Belichick did Shanahan a favor by trading him Jimmy Garoppolo for just a second round pick. Clearly he respected the young coach (and his father, a friend and ally of his), but he also probably calculated that the Niners were about the safest place to dump a QB he valued highly and reportedly wanted to make the successor to Tom Brady.

Belichick may have wanted to do Mike Shanahan's kid a favor, but just as likely he figured there was no way Garoppolo was going to pose a threat to the Patriots, given the 49ers' bad front line (at the time of the trade) and untested leadership team.

You couldn't blame the Dark Lord for thinking that, if he planned to coach for maybe 3 or 4 more years, then he had no realistic risk of facing San Francisco in any Super Bowl.

This was a team in the other conference that was 0-8 at the time of the trade, under a rookie coach and a rookie GM who'd had a shaky first draft. A team that was 2-14 the year before and had lost a ton of talent after coach Harbaugh's departure. At his age, there was no way he was going to ever face them in a Super Bowl.

If that was what he had been thinking, Belichick had to know by mid-October of 2019 that he had miscalculated badly. He had handed a potential rival the perfect weapon for their arsenal, and they were headed towards a showdown. Oops!

The cliché is that defense wins playoff games, and these two teams had by far the best defenses in football, by miles. No one else was even close.

This was no surprise for New England, but the leap that San Francisco had made was astounding. As I wrote at the time:

> *"Defense wins in the playoffs, and these undefeated teams are dominating the NFL defensively. They're also insanely close, statistically. The Patriots are giving up the fewest yards per game this year at 223.14 YPG. The Niners yield 223.50 YPG, just a third of a yard behind.*
> *To illustrate how dominant those numbers are, number 3 out of 32 teams is the Buffalo Bills — at 292.66 yards per game, 69 yards (31%) more. Only one other team (Denver) is under 325 YPG."* [62]

Belichick didn't just notice San Francisco; he made a move to restock, in preparation for a potential Super Bowl showdown. John Lynch did the same. Both New England

and San Francisco had excellent defenses but less than stellar wide receiving corps, and they both started looking for ways to upgrade before the trading deadline.

Both teams were probably also thinking about the New Orleans Saints, the strongest team in the NFC, who had matched their typically strong offense with an increasingly potent D -- but they were much stronger against the run than the pass.

San Francisco had the Saints coming up on their schedule, and knew that any playoff run would go through New Orleans. New England saw them as a potential Super Bowl rival. A beefier air attack would be important for either team to hold the Saints off.

As with offensive tackles, there weren't too many options available. One of them was an obvious choice for San Francisco -- the Falcons' Mohamed Sanu, a tall (6'2") but not especially fast (4.67) journeyman receiver who had never topped 850 yards in 8 NFL years. He did however play under Kyle Shanahan in his final year in Atlanta, going to the Super Bowl along with the rest of that team.

Before San Francisco could make a deal, though, Bill Belichick snatched him away in return for a 2020 second-round pick. This probably frustrated Lynch and Shanahan, though in retrospect they dodged a bullet and New England overpaid. Sanu was a disappointment, gaining only 207 yards in the final 8 games of the season.

Instead, the Niners got Denver Broncos wide receiver Emmanuel Sanders, a better receiver with a Super Bowl ring who ended up gaining more than 500 yards for San Francisco during the rest of the regular season and another 71 in the playoffs, despite playing 17 straight regular season games without a bye week.

I coined the nickname Emmanuel "Burny" Sanders for him, because he burns defenses (get it?). The nickname hasn't caught on yet because the world is a cesspit of cruelty and despair, but any day now....

Sanders' mid-season transition to the Niners' system was eased because he was playing in a very similar scheme -- Denver's offensive coordinator was Rich Scangarello, the Niners quarterbacks coach in 2017-8. He had been an offensive quality control coach under Kyle Shanahan in Atlanta in 2015, too.

The trade cost was less, too. San Francisco gave up their third-round and fourth-round picks in 2020. Better yet, they got in return the Bronco's fifth-round pick, which as we've seen is worth as much or more than a first or second round pick in John Lynch's hands for mysterious reasons.

There was a big asterisk, however: Sanders (like Jimmy Garoppolo at the time of his trade) was in the final year of his contract, and would become a free agent at the end of the year. At age 32, would the 49ers want to pay the kind of free agent money that a player on playoff team would get if he played well, in the spotlight?

Maybe not. But that's almost better, since San Francisco is likely to get a 3rd round comp pick for Sanders if he's signed away in free agency. So the deal would then be basically Denver's 5th-round pick (middle of the round) for San Francisco's 4th round pick (at the end of the round.)

Week 8. Carolina Panthers

If the horrible conditions and mounting injuries made the game in Washington a chore, week 8 was a return to joy and fun -- for the Niners anyway. It's unlikely that any Carolina fans felt good about this one.

San Francisco won 51-13, and amazingly, that score does not do justice to San Francisco's dominance. The score was 14-3 after one quarter, 27-3 at halftime, and 41-13 after three. Carolina only scored 3 times, and one of them was a safety.

The Panthers had entered the game on a wave of momentum, coming off of a bye week after winning four straight games with backup quarterback Kyle Allen at the helm, after Cam Newton was injured. Allen had never thrown an interception in 153 career pass attempts, and fans were predicting a quarterback controversy when Newton returned.

Oops.

Nick Bosa was dominant with 3 sacks, 9 pressures, an interception and 4 tackles. On his second sack, his bull rush lifted rookie tackle Dennis Daley up in the air, off both of his feet.

His interception was spectacular. Bosa sidestepped an attempted cut block by Daley, pushed down on the rookie's shoulders to maintain his balance, then jumped up just as Kyle Allen threw the pass. He high-pointed the pass perfectly, then broke 3 tackles as he ran it back for 46 yards after the catch, down to the 7 yard line. It was one of three San Francisco interceptions on the day.

Those statistics somehow understate his contribution, though, since the rookie was double-teamed on 13 snaps -- so he helped his teammates get through on those plays without marking the scorecard. On four of those double-teams, Christian McCaffrey stayed back to deliver a solid chip on Bosa, which took McCaffrey (Carolina's biggest offensive weapon) out of the play as a receiver.

On offense, Tevin Coleman reminded fans why the Niners signed him, with 4 touchdowns (one short of Jerry Rice's 49ers single game record). Newly acquired WR Emmanuel Sanders caught two passes on his first drive as a Niner, including a 4-yard touchdown.
If you think this account is biased in favor of the Niners, then listen to what the hometown newspaper (the Charlotte Observer) had to say. The headline is a bit of a spoiler: "**Panthers expected 49ers' misdirection, but still baffled and bamboozled in blowout.**"

> *"After spending the entire week preparing for the confusing deception of Kyle Shanahan's offense, the Panthers only nailed down the confused part, getting rolled over on their way to a 24-point halftime deficit and 51-13 loss on Sunday."*
>
> ...

> The Panthers had three points at that point
> [12:43 of the 2nd quarter, when the 49ers scored their
> third touchdown] and zero clue how to read the San
> Francisco offense, a cornucopia of draws and screens
> and play actions and clever misdirections. When the
> Panthers played zig, the 49ers had long ago zagged."
> 63

Matt Breida left the game after injuring his ankle, but the team was still undefeated and doing a pretty darned good job of slogging through the Staley, McGlinchey and Juszczyk injuries, running out the schedule until they could return, healthy. (Knock on wood.)

The backup tackles were doing a pretty solid job -- at least Daniel Brunskill was -- and having a healthy George Kittle meant there was still a lot of excellent blocking left in the lineup.

Pass Target Diversity

By this point, it was halfway through the season, and I saw a statistic on Twitter after the Panthers game that I couldn't believe was true, courtesy of someone named Joe Lami:

> "With Coleman & Sanders each catching a TD today, Garoppolo has now thrown 9 TDs to 9 different receivers on the year." 64

> **Joe Lami**
> @joe_lami
>
> With Coleman & Sanders each catching a TD today, Garoppolo has now thrown 9 TDs to 9 different receivers on the year. #49ers #GoNiners
>
> ♡ 3   5:23 PM - Oct 27, 2019

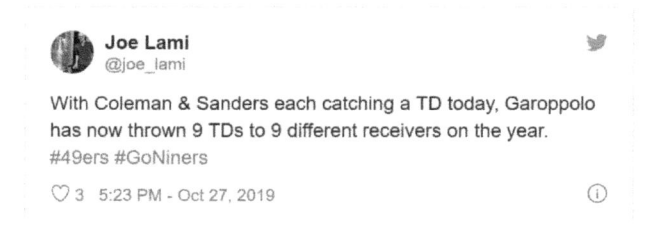

Granted, that's not a lot of touchdowns for a half a season, which makes sense given the Niners' tremendous running game. There was a lot of criticism of the team and of Garoppolo, that they couldn't pass, that Shanahan was hiding his weakness, that the team needed a "true WR1."

And there was clearly some truth to that, given all of the injuries. Juszczyk is the Niners best pass protecting blocker on third down. With Juice and the best three offensive tackles out injured, it makes sense that Shanahan would prefer to avoid drop backs wherever possible.

But my thoughts ran the other way -- how was it possible that a QB who didn't pass much had thrown touchdowns to nine different targets? I looked it up, and the numbers checked out. Here's what I wrote at the time:

> *"Garoppolo has not thrown two TDs to any target. And you will never convince me that this is an accident.*
> *Four of the people catching touchdowns aren't even wide receivers: George Kittle, Raheem Mostert, Tevin Coleman, and Matt Breida. In fact, 4th string RB Jeff Wilson, Jr. and 5th string WR Kendrick Bourne are the only backs who haven't caught touchdowns this year, and they probably will later.*

> So let's say you're a defensive coordinator scheming up a game plan. Who should your best CB (say, Stephon Gilmore) cover? Gilmore, like the Rams' Jalen Ramsey, wants to play the offense's best receiver — but who is that?
>
> George Kittle? Emmanuel Sanders, now? Whatever. Shanahan can send that target deep, on the far side of the field, and attack the rest of the turf with four other targets, safely away from him because every single skill player on the Niners is a good receiver. ...
>
> So fret not, Niners faithful. The passing game isn't weak. It's waiting." [65]

Kendrick Bourne caught a touchdown pass later that same day, against Arizona, to provide the winning margin. And one week later, he became the first San Francisco receiver to catch a second TD in 2019.

On November 17th -- three weeks hence -- Wilson caught the game winner against Arizona. Always the target you expect the least.

Week 9. Arizona Cardinals

After all the success they had despite a bad rash of injuries, including eight straight victories, the Niners could be forgiven for overlooking the Arizona Cardinals, the only team that had a worse record than them in 2018. If they did, it almost cost them the game.

Arizona jumped out to a quick 7-0 lead, and even after San Francisco appeared to put the game away, the Cardinals came roaring back.

Rookie Kyler Murray gave the Niners reason to worry about their upcoming game against Seattle, showing a scrambling, evasive game like Russell Wilson's but with more aggressive sliding when he did run.

Murray jumped down like a shortstop who'd just stolen second at the end of his runs, which makes sense since he was drafted by the Oakland A's and even signed a baseball contract before opting for football.

Coach Kliff Kingsbury was also a rookie, and figured to be a vulnerability for the Cardinals since he was unemployed and had been fired from his last college coaching gig when Arizona hired him. As it turned out he proved impressive all year, but made one key mistake in this game that betrayed his inexperience.

San Francisco had the ball, 4th and goal at the Arizona one-yard line, and Jeff Wilson Jr. got stuffed to end the half -- except that Kingsbury had called a time out right before the play started, to "get a snapshot" of the Niners' play, he later said.

Garoppolo got a second chance and threw for a touchdown to go up 21-7. That was one of four touchdowns he threw, quieting some of the "game manager" talk he was getting.

San Francisco hadn't needed to pass much before this game, but now they did, and Jimmy G did pretty darned well for himself: 28-37 for 317 yards.

Just as importantly, he was great at running out the clock in the 4-minute offense after Andy Isabella scored on a long run after a short pass to cut the lead to three.

To be precise, Garoppolo burned the final 4:53 off the clock in taking the Niners from their own 26 to Arizona's 37. That included two clutch completions on 3rd and long, one to backup tight end Ross Dwelley, and the other to Emmanuel Sanders, who was wasting no time in proving his value to the Niners.

Injuries, giant piles of injuries

George Kittle took a helmet to his knee, but returned to the game later and even scored a touchdown. However, he was indeed injured, which explains Dwelley's presence on a third down, and was lost for weeks.

That wasn't all. Linebacker Kwon Alexander tore his pectoral muscle and was lost for the rest of the season, it appeared. (See separate article.)

Dee Ford hurt his quadriceps muscle and played only sparingly the rest of the regular season. This was a big loss, because he and Nick Bosa strengthened each others' games mightily. For the rest of the regular season, the team not only missed Ford's sacks, but Bosa's sacks faded into pressures in Ford's absence.

Kicker Robbie Gould also hurt his quadriceps muscle, forcing the team to sign a rookie (Chase McLaughlin) who had played a few games in injury relief for San Diego, making six of nine field goals.

San Francisco was now missing several key defenders as well as its top five blockers -- the three tackles, Juszczyk and Kittle -- going into the toughest part of its schedule.

One bright spot who kept things from getting worse was rookie tackle Daniel Brunskill. (See separate article.)

The fifth tackle on San Francisco's roster, he was forced to start, and had to line up across from players such as Michael Brockers of the Rams and Gerald McCoy of the Panthers.

He not only survived, but he also made Pro Football Focus' team of the week against Carolina with a grade of 79.7, as the Niners picked up 232 yards rushing. Brunskill put himself in position to be considered as a future starting tackle, and established himself as the team's leading reserve lineman.

All-Pro left tackle Joe Staley is 35, and obviously doesn't have that many good years left. If the team can replace him without drafting or trading, that would free up huge resources for other positions. The team spent a first round pick (#9 overall) on their other tackle, Mike McGlinchey, and no one is criticizing that choice.

Feels great, baby

After the game, sideline reporter Erin Andrews asked the victorious Jimmy G how it felt to have an 8-0 record. He flashed a sly smile and said "Feels great, baby." Andrews appeared to be caught off guard by the response and perhaps even blushed.

(For the record, Garoppolo is famously handsome, sometimes compared to a young George Clooney, and Andrews is not hard on the eyes herself.)

Social media loved it, taking the quarterback's response as flirting. Fans tweeted "Shoot your shot, Jimmy!" and T-shirts with the phrase became hot sellers.

Garoppolo's agent filed for a trademark for the phrase, and at his press conference after the week 17 game against Seattle, George Kittle appeared wearing a t-shirt with that slogan. (He later appeared wearing a t-shirt featuring a picture of Garoppolo, shirtless.)

Garoppolo downplayed the whole thing, though, saying he called everyone "baby," male or female, and his teammates backed him up on the point. Before the NFC Championship game, she interviewed him again and brought it up again to clear the air.

"They are all in on the Jimmy G vibe here, right? I mean, how does that feel? Feels great, right?" [66]

Nick Bosa Plants the Flag

-- Akash Anavarathan

"He had it coming. I just wanted to get payback. I think everybody knows what it was for."

Nick Bosa proclaimed this with a slight smirk to the media after the Cleveland game.

This story goes all the way back to late September 2017 in Columbus, OH. It was a heavyweight Week 2 matchup in the Horseshoe featuring Baker Mayfield's Oklahoma State against Nick Bosa's Ohio State.

Mayfield and Co. pulled off a huge upset victory on the road and it didn't stop there. After the game, Mayfield ran around the stadium waving an Oklahoma State flag, then literally planted it into the turf in the middle of the big O at mid-field at Ohio Stadium.

The Buckeyes were already in the locker room and unable to respond; had they been on the field, a brawl would likely have broken out.

In the Bosa household, there's clearly no statute of limitations on how long one can hold a grudge. Now let's fast forward two years to October 2019. Mayfield and the Browns are coming into Levi's Stadium for a huge *Monday Night Football* showdown against rookie Nick Bosa's 49ers.

The preseason hype train on the Browns was fully packed and they were the favorites to win the NFC North. They were 2-2 coming into the 49ers game and looking to establish a rhythm amidst a tough stretch in their schedule. On the flip side, San Francisco was 3-0 and were trying to tally their best win of the season, after beating Tampa Bay, Cincinnati and a Ben Roethlisberger-less Steelers.

On the opening play, 49ers' running back Matt Breida was off to the races with a 83-yard touchdown run and San Francisco would not look back. They jumped out to a 21-3 halftime lead and pounded on the Browns, 31-3.

The game was the first sign that the San Francisco 49ers were for real – but the win itself was not the highlight of the Week 5 matchup.

The highlight wasn't Richard Sherman's interception against Baker Mayfield or George Kittle's receiving touchdown. No, the brightest moment of the game came at the hands of the No. 2 overall pick – who had a coming out party on national television in front of a grand audience.

Late in the fourth quarter, on a second-and-12 play from the Cleveland 16-yard line, Mayfield took the snap and was immediately bottled up by Bosa, who forced the ball out of the quarterback's hands.

While the Levi's crowd was loudly celebrating Bosa's second sack of the game, the former Ohio State pass rusher had a little revenge on his mind.

The No. 2 overall pick ran towards the north end zone, carrying an invisible flag which he planted directly into turf -- and into what remained of Baker Mayfield's heart.

It wasn't a spur of the moment decision by the former Ohio State defensive end. During the Week 4 bye, Bosa worked out with former Ohio State defender Sam Hubbard and mentioned the possibility of a flag plant celebration to him.

The flag plant during the game wasn't the first time Bosa had done that celebration. He had practiced it all week in the hotel just to make sure he would get it right.

That was not the end of it, either.

Bosa is not known to be a trash talker during games, but he kept talking to the Browns' quarterback for the rest of the game. "Baaaa-ker. Baaaa-ker. Pick it up, we want a challenge," was one of the greetings Bosa shared throughout their 31-3 beat down of the Browns.

Mayfield was asked about the flag plant celebration and he responded "Good for him. Good play."

Bosa had been absolutely dominant in this game, racking up four tackles, two sacks and a forced fumble. The rookie had missed all of preseason and fans were nervous about his prior injury history.

And it's true that his lingering ankle issue limited his effectiveness during the first three games of the season. With a boost from the bye week and motivation from their personal history, the Cleveland game gave Nick Bosa his first chance to show how dominant he can be in one of the season's signature moments.

Richard Sherman, Chippiness and Motivation

-- Mark Saltveit

Professional football players are hyper-competitive as a rule, and the occasional exceptions tend to wash out of the NFL pretty quickly.

Coaches and fans alike are well aware of the danger of creating locker room bulletin board material before a game -- the boasting, challenges to manhood, or insults that motivate opponents to compete even harder.

But the amount of energy that Richard Sherman generates from what he sees as disrespect or slights is unmatched. And it has pushed him further in a career almost certain to end in the Hall of Fame.

It's not that he's always fighty or cocky. He often shares respect with worthy opponents who return the favor, as he did with Kansas City Chiefs speedster Mecole Hardman before they faced off in the Super Bowl.

But if you don't respect Sherman or his team, well, deal with the consequences. He first came to the broader public's attention with his rant against then-Niner Michael Crabtree after he breaking up a potential game-winning touchdown pass in the 2013 NFC Championship game.

He was obviously responding to some disrespectful analysis about his coverage skills (or perhaps his mother) that Crabtree had delivered before that crucial play, but the people at home never saw that part.

Sherman's response was broadcast to tens of millions of people who had never had a direct shot of competitive player trash-talk before, and many fans were frightened by Sherman's intensity (as well as, frankly, in many cases just racist).

We've already discussed Sherman's response to Adam Rank's dismissal of the Niners as a 3-13 team, but notice how central the concept of integrity is to his challenge.

> *"...don't flip-flop with us. If you said we weren't going to make it, if you said we were some way early on, stick with that position. ... Stick by your word."*

There was a huge dustup after the Cleveland game, when Sherman told Michael Silver of NFL.com that Baker Mayfield had refused to shake his hand at the coin toss, and that motivated the team to put the cocky youngster in his place. [67]

Fans started reviewing the tape and found the place where Mayfield and Sherman sort of slapped hands, filling talk radio for hours and hours with their hot takes on the matter.

Sherman ended up apologizing to Baker publicly and privately, but a couple of things about the incident were lost in all the shouting.

First, Mayfield *was* pretty brash and cocky, especially his rookie year, and many pundits hyped him as an MVP candidate before the 2019 season. If you watch the video of the hand-slap, [68] it was kind of jokey and dismissive on Mayfield's part -- unlike the more serious and respectful handshake Sherman shared with Cleveland LB Adarius Taylor immediately afterwards.

In the Silver article, the cornerback lists several other obnoxious bits of behavior from the rookie, such as criticizing his teammate Duke Johnson, mocking his ex-coach Hue Jackson on the football field after Jackson took a job with Cincinnati, and trashing the pick of Daniel Jones by New York.

Second, Sherman was not the only Niner who didn't like Mayfield's attitude. Remember, this was Nick Bosa's "plant the flag" revenge game against the rookie quarterback. Bosa told Silver that

> *"I've been mad for two years. And I was gonna get him back tonight."*

Third and most importantly, the motivation worked. Sherman and Bosa *did* put Mayfield in his place, and he was less cocky (and less successful) for the rest of the 2019 season.

When Richard Sherman started his pro career back in 2011, there was no ambiguity about some of the slights *he* faced, as David Lombardi detailed in an article for the Athletic that's well worth looking up. [69]

At the Senior Bowl, for example, Sherman got beat on a double move while trying to ballhawk, and while he recovered in time to break up the pass, he remembers his coach (Cincinnati's Marvin Lewis) yelling at him afterwards.

> *"That's why you're not getting drafted. That's why you're not going to f**king play in this league!"*

Lombardi recounts that Sherman kept quiet but thought:

> *"OK, you don't know who the f**k you're talking to, but I hear you. You're the coach, so I can't say sh*t to you right now, but I usually get my revenge. And I'm gonna get my revenge."*

Jump ahead to Sherman's first NFL start, and sure enough, it's against the Bengals, coached by Lewis. And the rookie's memory of disrespect wasn't the only thing that motivated him.

Sherman was matched up against WR A.J. Green, who started trash talking the rookie, like you do.

> *"I'm better than you. I was drafted fifth pick [overall] and I'm about to show you why."*

The combined disrespect from both Green and coach Lewis only fueled Sherman, at least the way he tells the story.

> *"I'm nervous. It's my first game. But you sent me to a place where my nervousness and anxiety is out the window, because you got me to a place where all I'm doing is trying to embarrass you now for the rest of the game. And I don't give a f**k about anything else.*
>
> *And with that, I don't think about anything. My*

> *will power kicks in. Will is much different than preparation or athleticism. Will, it's very hard to overcome when I'm willful in that way."* ...

Don't think for a second that Sherman forgot about coach Lewis' insults, either.

> *"I got a pick on his team that he's coaching, in front of his bench. And I threw the ball right at him, like, 'You f**king bitch. Don't you ever talk about me.' That was my first career pick."*

The nuance about all of this, and the thing missed by so many "hot takes" on this Baker Mayfield handshake brouhaha, is that Sherman absolutely believes these slights are real. And he really doesn't care whether you do or not.

He's not trying to ruin anyone's reputation. He's trying to destroy his opponents on the field, and he's psyching himself up in the way that works best.

After he apologized to Mayfield, he said

> *"That's what I thought happened. That's what I remembered happening. He stood back and I said it the way I remembered it happening. I took it as disrespect and I took it out on him, as I should."* [70]

And if Sherman is maybe less skeptical about his perceptions than a good customer service employee should be, or less than gracious about incidents of understandable human miscommunication, well good for him. Placebos actually work, too, even if they don't have an active ingredient. That's the definition of a placebo.

Whatever the facts behind Adam Rank's disrespect or Baker Mayfield's attitude at the coin toss, they drove him to be his best. And at 31, coming off of a torn Achilles tendon that caused Seattle to simply cut him, Sherman won PFF's award as 2019's Top Coverage Defender. [71]

Emmanuel Moseley

-- Akash Anavarathan

Given the salary cap restrictions and the demand at the position, it's really difficult for teams to have two good corners on the outside. Think about it – how many teams in the NFL currently employ multiple defensive backs that are playing at a high level?

Luckily for the 49ers, they have Hall-of-Fame bound Richard Sherman on one side and underrated K'Waun Williams in the slot during nickel packages, but the third corner was a weakness in the 49ers' defense in the first two years of the Lynch-Shanahan regime.

It was an area that general manager John Lynch addressed during the 2019 offseason, signing ex-Chargers' CB Jason Verrett and drafting Virginia's Tim Harris to fix the turnstile at the second outside corner position. Incumbents Ahkello Witherspoon and Emmanuel Moseley would also be a part of the competition for the starting job.

Witherspoon won the battle during the preseason, aided by injuries to Harris that would sideline him for the entire 2019 season. Three weeks into the season, Witherspoon himself went down with an injury that put him on the bench until Week 11.

Verrett stepped in for Witherspoon, but he allowed 81 yards on two plays, including a 38-yard touchdown, and it became abundantly clear that the former Charger wasn't going to be a long-term answer at corner.

After seeing Verrett's struggles, the 49ers had no chance but to turn over the reins to second-year undrafted player Emmanuel Moseley. Moseley was overlooked in the draft in part because at 5'11", he lacked the height that GMs prefer in outside cornerbacks. Then, during his rookie season, he was injured for the rest of the season almost as soon as he was called up to the active roster.

As a starter from Week 5 to Week 12, while Witherspoon was injured, Moseley outperformed everyone's expectation.

Outside of an 88-yard reception that the former UDFA allowed against the Cardinals in Week 9, Moseley was effective in coverage, especially considering that he was getting quarterbacks' primary attention playing opposite Richard Sherman. He also excelled as a tackler, something his stout, 190-pound frame is well suited to.

Many assumed that the former Tennessee cornerback would continue to hold onto his starting job when Witherspoon returned, but Robert Saleh and defensive backs coach Joe Woods favored the veteran over Moseley.

After Witherspoon's return, the two cornerbacks would rotate in and out depending on the game situation and how they performed in that specific moment.

After the Falcons' game, I caught up with the ex-Tennessee corner in the locker room and spoke to him about how he and Witherspoon handle the rotation. The 49ers were without Richard Sherman that game, and Moseley was matched up against Julio Jones (who absolutely shredded the 49ers' pass defense, as he tends to do).

Moseley hammered home that it was about "next man up mentality" and that "the team will watch the film, figure out how to get better and then improve ahead of next week's matchup."

But Moseley's importance wasn't fully seen until the opening round of the playoffs. In the divisional round, the 49ers faced off against the Vikings, who feature multiple capable receivers in Adam Thielen and Stefon Diggs.

Kirk Cousins and the Vikings' passing game feared Richard Sherman so they went right after Witherspoon – who gave up multiple third-down conversions and a critical penalty, then fell down on a touchdown throw to Diggs.

"I have a lot of faith in Ahkello and I have a lot of faith in E-Man," the 49ers' head coach claimed after the game. But actions speak louder than words.

Woods, Saleh and Shanahan clearly had Ahkello on a short leash, and didn't hesitate one bit before benching him after the ugly series. Moseley quickly settled things down. He ended up with 2 pass breakups, keeping pace with Richard Sherman (who had 1 PBU and 1 interception), and adding 5 solo tackles to lead all defensive backs.

While the NFL is filled with divas that would normally be upset that they were benched during the middle of a playoff game, the 49ers' culture doesn't embrace that type of behavior. Instead of sulking or being resentful, Witherspoon went to San Francisco's special teams' coordinator Richard Hightower and asked for all of Moseley's special teams snaps so that the new starter could focus all of his energy on defense.

Wow. I hadn't heard of a player making such a request to a coach before, but it characterizes the selflessness of this 2019 49ers' team beautifully.

Shanahan wouldn't announce a starter before the NFC Championship game, but it became obvious as the week went on that Moseley would be the starter, not the former third-round pick.

Once again, the un-drafted free agent stepped up. He had 4 solo tackles, a pass breakup, and a tackle for loss. Moseley also grabbed an interception against Aaron Rodgers, a quarterback famous for protecting the ball at all costs, which led to a San Francisco touchdown right before halftime and a dominating 27-0 lead.

Rodgers tested Moseley five times and completed three of those but for only 34 yards total.[72]

After an exceptional performance, Moseley retained his starting spot for the Super Bowl, but the challenge would be on a different scale, guarding the likes of Tyreek Hill, Mecole Hardman and Sammy Watkins against the NFL's best young quarterback.

Moseley gave up six catches on eight targets, but his biggest mistake came in the Super Bowl's most crucial moment. On third-and-15 late in the fourth quarter, the Chiefs were desperate to keep the drive – and their Super Bowl hopes – alive.

Saleh called for a Cover-3, which meant that Moseley had to cover a deep third, but the Chiefs' offensive coordinator Eric Bieniemy called a play designed specifically to challenge the cornerback in his position.

Sammy Watkins ran a vertical route near the sideline in Moseley's zone while Tyreek Hill appeared to be crossing into safety Jimmie Ward's center zone. This forced the youngster to choose which one he would cover.

As soon as he focused on Watkins, Hill cut back into Moseley's zone, way behind him. Jimmie Ward, playing the center-field role, couldn't get over in time to break up the pass.

It's fair to criticize Moseley for playing it safe on 3rd-and-long, but to be fair this is a great play specifically designed to challenge this coverage. This same play was the only long pass Kansas City completed against the New England Patriots' elite secondary in the 2018 AFC Championship Game, so Moseley is at least in good company.

The corner is going to be a free agent at the end of the season, but his performance this season should give the 49ers every reason to bring him back. His toughness, open-field tackling ability and coverage against receivers during the season is only going to get better with an offseason against the first-team offense.

Chapter 6. November

vs. Seattle, November 11th, 2019
49ers lose (in overtime), 24-27

vs. Arizona, November 17th, 2019
49ers win, 36-26

vs. Green Bay, November 24th, 2019
49ers win, 37-8

Winning or losing games in football always involves a certain amount of luck, with the subjective nature of refereeing, the chaos of 22 huge men slamming into each other, and the erratic way that the oval ball bounces (literally). But going undefeated is an astonishing achievement.

In some ways, the New England Patriot's 16-0 season was more impressive than their Super Bowl wins, even though they lost the big game on a last-minute pass. Being better than all of your opponents is not enough, because the odds work against you.

Let's say you have an 80% chance of winning every single game -- you're that dominant. Those odds multiply, though, so you only have a 64% chance of winning two of those in a row (80% of 80%). The odds of 3 in a row are barely above even (51.2%, to be exact).

By the time you get to 8 games in a row, the odds of that dominant (80%) team winning all of them has dropped to 16.78%, and no one would have said the 49ers had an 80% chance of winning any *one* of their 2019 games, much less all of them.

And the odds of winning all 16? Just 2.81%. That's what makes the Patriots' 2007 achievement so special.

How did San Francisco manage to win 8 in a row coming off a 4-12 season? Mostly defense, as the offense's power was largely poured into surviving all of its injuries. As November rolled around, though, the defense started picking up its own share of casualties.

Greg Bishop explained in Sports Illustrated:

"In the first eight weeks of this potentially Super season, the 49ers defense allowed 11 points a game on average, and San Francisco ranked first in QBR allowed, sacks, sack rate and passing yards allowed.
But injuries befell the unit. Ford hurt his quadriceps, Bosa tweaked an ankle, Alexander tore a pec and Sherman strained his hamstring." [73]

Week 10: Seattle Seahawks

Russell Wilson has been a Niners-killer for years, and even though the rest of his roster has been depleted, it's impossible to ever feel comfortable about facing a team with him at quarterback.

Have you ever tried to kick a pigeon? Not only is it impossible, but they make it extra aggravating by jump out of the way by the smallest possible margin, as if taunting you: "Oh! Almost got me, big guy! Try again, see what happens."

That's what it's like watching your defensive linemen try to sack Wilson.

This game was a heavyweight prize fight, going to overtime, but ultimately the tide of injuries drowned the Niners. Notably, George Kittle was out, and a rib injury forced top wide receiver Emmanuel Sanders to the bench in the first quarter.

Jadeveon Clowney terrorized Garoppolo, who suffered five sacks and threw 24 for 48, for 248 yards. Defensive linemen on both teams (Clowney and DeForest Buckner) scored on fumble returns.

San Francisco led early, but Wilson found TE Jacob Hollister, a favorite target, on first and goal at the three to take a 14-10 lead.
It was back and forth for the rest of the game.

A surprising hero was substitute kicker Chase McLaughlin who made 3 field goals in regulation to keep San Francisco in the game, including a 47-yarder with one second remaining to tie it at 24.

In overtime, rookie linebacker Dre Greenlaw, replacing the injured Kwon Alexander's, made a huge play by intercepting Russell Wilson at San Francisco's 4 yard-line. A Seattle touchdown would have ended the game.

To put that in perspective, Wilson was in the middle of the best season of his career, statistically. This was only his second interception of the entire season -- in week 10. And then Greenlaw returned the ball 47 yards to midfield.

But Chase McLaughlin's short career as a 49ers hero ended abruptly when he missed a 47-yard field goal would have won the game. (He shanked it way left.)

Predictably, Russell Wilson led a killer drive after McLaughlin's miss, scrambling for 18 yards on 3rd-and-3, and Jason Meyers hit a 42-yard field goal to win.

Week 11: Arizona Cardinals

After two tough games in a row and several more 49ers injuries, Arizona was not looking like the easy win they had figured to be when the schedule was first announced. Especially not on a short week, playing on Thursday night.

George Kittle was still out. Emmanuel Sanders played but was still limited from injury. In their absence, Deebo Samuel romped for 134 yards and Kyle Juszczyk caught 7 passes (on 7 targets) for 63 more.

Not surprisingly, Arizona once again dared Jimmy G to pass, holding the Niners to 34 yards on the ground, and once again he responded: 4 touchdowns, 424 yards on 34-45 passing, though he had two bad (red zone) interceptions. The only other 49ers quarterbacks to ever throw 400 yards and 4 touchdowns in a game were named Joe Montana and Steve Young.

But this game was even closer than the first game against Arizona. The final margin of victory that time was 3 points, but this margin was padded by a fumble runback for a touchdown after the final play, when Arizona botched a desperation multi-lateral play.

The Niners fell behind early 16-0 as the offense stalled, and they trailed 23-26 with six and a half minutes left after Kyler Murray scored on a 22-yard keeper.

But Garoppolo led a touchdown drive that culminated in a 25-yard touchdown to reserve running back Jeff Wilson, Jr.

It was the running back's first snap of the game, and you may recall that he was the only one of the 49ers' top 11 skill players who had not caught a touchdown pass this season. (Add a twelfth: backup tight end Ross Dwelley caught two touchdowns in this game.)

Since Wilson Jr. was not considered a receiving threat, Arizona had edge rusher Chandler Jones covering him on the play, probably figuring he was going to stay in for pass protection. Instead Wilson, Jr. put a quick move on the big man, who wasn't agile enough to keep up and actually fell down on the play.

This was San Francisco's biggest comeback since 2012.

All this victory did was set up heavily injured San Francisco to run what everyone was calling The Gauntlet (three consecutive games against 8-2 Green Bay, 9-2 Baltimore and 10-2 New Orleans). Despite San Francisco's 9-1 record, the odds said they would be lucky to win one of the three.

Whatever the outcome, it would certainly answer the critics who kept asking, "Who have they played?"

Week 12. Green Bay Packers

Thanksgiving indeed.

Facing elite quarterback Aaron Rodgers and his star receiver Davante Adams, San Francisco had all the answers on offense and defense. It got out of hand quickly for the Packers, as Fred Warner strip-sacked Rodgers on the opening drive for a turnover at the two-yard line, and Tevin Coleman ran it in on the next play.

George Kittle was back, as he illustrated with a 61-yard touchdown in the third quarter. Rookie Deebo Samuel showed his growth with a 42-yard touchdown of his own, part of ten points the Niners scored in the final two minutes before halftime.

Overall, Garoppolo was 14 of 20 for 253 yards and no turnovers. Not the big statistical game he had against Arizona the week before, but a model of efficiency.

Hot and cold cornerback Ahkello Witherspoon shut down Davante Adams, sometimes with the help of bracket coverage from safety Jimmie Ward. The Niners had 12 tackles for loss, including a stuff of RB Aaron Jones on 4th and 1 for a turnover on downs.

Aaron Rodgers had one of the worst games of his long career, something that happened to a lot of quarterbacks who played San Francisco this season. He managed just 104 yards, 20-33 and was sacked five times. In fact, Rodgers was benched for the last five minutes of the game, as backup Tim Boyle ran the last 11 plays with a higher passer rating.

The final score was 37-8 San Francisco, about as good a start for this tough 3-game stretch as could be hoped for.

Late season losses vs. Seattle and Baltimore

-- Akash Anavarathan

"Feels great, baby," Jimmy Garoppolo said to FOX's Erin Andrews, as the 49ers put together a heroic performance down in the desert against the Cardinals in Week 9 to keep their undefeated season alive.

Garoppolo had just carried the team to a tremendous road victory, throwing for 317 yards and four touchdowns, on a short week. San Francisco had just capped off a miraculous 8-0 start and were about to put an undefeated record up against their arch rival – the Seattle Seahawks.

The 49ers were about to enter a brutal stretch in their schedule. Up until that point, they were mostly sleepwalking through the games, handily beating their opponents, but the pressure was now cranked up to a ten on the meter.

This stretch would reveal the true potential of this 49ers' team – were they pretenders or to be taken seriously as contenders?

Normally before the season begins, when the NFL releases the schedule, I always do two things: highlight all the 49ers' primetime games, and circle the two 49ers-Seahawks' matchups in bold ink.

This time, though, there was something more ominous in the schedule, often referred to in the Bay Area as "The

Gauntlet." The 49ers were going to face four playoff teams in their next five games – including two on the road in noisy, hostile stadiums.

If the 49ers could finish this stretch at 3-2, it would be seen as an enormous achievement given the difficulty of their opponents and the travel schedule.

San Francisco had 11 days to prepare for Seattle, a mini-bye going from a Thursday night game to Monday Night Football, and they were playing at home in Levi's Stadium. The 49ers were finally relevant again and their fans were excited for a competitive game against the hated (and dreaded) Seahawks.

The 49ers were going to be without tight end George Kittle who had a bone injury, though starting tackles Mike McGlinchey and Joe Staley made their return to the lineup after missing time with various injuries.

Another pivotal injury struck kicker Robbie Gould, which meant that John Lynch had to sign kicker Chase McLaughlin off the street mid-week.

Here's the thing with kickers – when they're hitting field goals and extra points, fans take them from granted and overlook their value. Yet, when the player starts missing kicks, it becomes a blatant weak link to the entire operation.

It's like a key cog in the engine that everybody takes for granted until it stops working, and then everyone freaks out about it.

The 11 days between the Cardinals' game and Seahawks' game felt like an eternity, especially for someone (such as me) who lives in Seattle and covers the 49ers. It felt like there was a heightened magnitude on this game and a rebirth of a rivalry.

All week long, the sense around the NFL was that another clash of the titans between the Seahawks and 49ers was brewing, after a hiatus since the 2014 exit of former head coach Jim Harbaugh.

San Francisco had been somewhat of a punching bag for Seattle between 2015 and 2018, but now was the chance for the 49ers to redeem themselves. They had more talent on paper, they were at home and they were the more rested team going into the game – all of which amplified their need to win.

Looming ahead on the schedule was a regular season finale rematch with Pete Carroll's team in the Pacific Northwest, so winning this game would be a huge help in case of a tiebreaker. You didn't want to put yourself in a situation where the Week 17 game at Century Link Field was a must-win if you could possibly avoid it.

San Francisco came flying out of the gates and punched Seattle in the mouth to open up to a 10-0 lead, which brought a raucous Monday night Levi's crowd to their feet. But the 49ers lost another player to injury – recently-acquired Emmanuel Sanders, who was beginning to impact the 49ers' passing game in a positive fashion.

That meant that the 49ers were left with Deebo Samuel and Kendrick Bourne as their primary receivers. That is not a whole lot of game experience against a veteran Seahawks' defense.

With injuries to Kittle and Sanders, San Francisco's passing attack struggled to get uncorked and Jimmy Garoppolo played one of his shakier games of the season. San Francisco found themselves down 21-10 heading into the fourth quarter and seemed to be staring down their first loss of the season.

Garoppolo would not let that happen, willing the offense through a 10-play, 40-yard drive with 1:45 on the game clock to force the game into overtime. Newly-signed kicker McLaughlin would play a huge role here, nailing a 47-yard field goal as time expired to send the game into extra time.

Russell Wilson had the ball to start the extra 10-minute. He sliced-and-diced the 49ers' banged-up defense, which was exhausted from four quarters of chasing Wilson around, and un able to rush the passer as effectively without Dee Ford.

With the game slipping away from the 49ers, rookie linebacker Dre Greenlaw (in his first start, by the way) made a fantastic play to intercept what looked like a certain touchdown pass, giving the 49ers' offense a chance to win this game.

"Three points. Find a way to get three." That's all I thought to myself. The 49ers' offense wasn't far from field-goal range, after Greenlaw's big return, and they just needed a way to get within McLaughlin's striking range.

After seven plays, the 49ers were only able to move the ball 20 yards and McLaughlin had a chance to etch his name into team history by hitting one kick to beat their arch rival on prime-time television.

The kicker's face displayed zero confidence as he walked on to take his second 47-yard field goal attempt. Just minutes before, McLaughlin had connected on a field goal from the same distance and side of the field to send the 49ers to overtime. Could he repeat it one more time?

Nope. The ball landed in the 49ers' locker room tunnel which is way, way, waaaay wide left of the uprights.

Reality began to set in for San Francisco. They had lost to their rivals and were facing three more playoff teams in the next four games, watching Seattle in the rear-view mirror with a slim lead in the NFC West.

The hangover from a Seattle game is real. The 49ers found themselves in a 16-0 deficit the following week against Kyler Murray and the Cardinals. Was the 49ers' magical eight-game win streak a product of their weak schedule rather than their sheer dominance?

The Levi's crowd tightened up, and nervousness filled the afternoon air in Santa Clara. The 49ers had to host Green Bay and then head to Baltimore and New Orleans in the next three weeks. This game against the Cardinals wasn't one they could afford to lose.

Jimmy Garoppolo wouldn't let them, throwing for 424 yards and 4 TDs at a 75.6% completion rate. Instead of a sudden 8-2, they moved to 9-1 and were confident heading into a show-down with the Green Bay Packers.

The NFL decided to make this the marquee matchup of the weekend, flexing it into *Sunday Night Football*, and the 49ers were going to host their first NBC Sunday night game since 2014.

Sadly, it wasn't what the NFL was hoping for when they pushed this matchup into primetime. Rodgers fumbled on the first drive of the game and the 49ers were on the board before fans took a sip of their first drink.

San Francisco put their foot on the Packers' throats and did not give them a chance to come up for air. It was a "you don't belong on the same field" performance from Kyle Shanahan's team against the second-best team in the conference.

Raheem Mostert, Tevin Coleman and the 49ers' rushing attack had a coming out party as they danced their way into the end zone. After missing multiple games, George Kittle returned to the tune of six catches, 129 yards and a huge touchdown run in the second half.

After the game, I spoke to Kittle about missing the last few games and watching from the Press Box, rather than being on the field with his teammates.

"Absolutely brutal," he responded, "so I'm going to do everything in my power to not do that ever again."

The locker room was as excited as I have seen it. Music blared and guys were smiling and enjoying themselves after a huge victory against one of the premier quarterbacks in the NFL in Aaron Rodgers.

Their work was still cut out for them, as the 49er headed out on the road for a two-week trip, deciding to stay in Florida in between their games against the Ravens and Saints.

San Francisco was sitting at 10-1, but they were going against the hottest team in football. The Ravens had just demolished the Rams on *Monday Night Football* and QB Lamar Jackson (the eventual MVP) was taking the league by storm.

The 49ers had struggled against Russell Wilson and Kyler Murray in previous games, fueling the concern that San Francisco wouldn't be able to stop Jackson's potent run game.

The forecast called for an ugly, rainy, monsoon-like atmosphere, which would negate the 49ers' new-found passing game and favor a ground-and-pound matchup that would benefit Baltimore.

Mostert rushed for 146 yards and controlled the ground game for the 49ers, who looked like they were going to escape Maryland with their 11th win of the season.

Saleh's defense gave up 101 rushing yards to Jackson – but he only threw for 105 yards, so the Ravens' high-flying offense was grounded on the tarmac for the afternoon.

It all came down to a fourth-and-one play on the Baltimore 35-yard line late in the fourth quarter. Kyle Shanahan could have elected to kick a 53-yard field goal late in the final period or gain the yard to keep the drive alive.

He chose to be aggressive and go for it, but a questionable pass to Kittle landed incomplete and the 49ers turned the ball over to Jackson and the Ravens with more than five minutes remaining.

The 49ers wouldn't touch the ball again, as Justin Tucker sealed a Baltimore victory and suddenly San Francisco's lead in the NFC West race seemed precarious, even with a 10-2 record.

Chapter 7. December

at Baltimore Ravens, December 1st, 2019
49ers lose, 17-20

at New Orleans Saints, December 8th, 2019
49ers win, 48-46

vs. Atlanta Falcons, December 15th, 2019
49ers lose, 22-29

vs. Los Angeles Rams, December 22nd, 2019
49ers win, 34-31

at Seattle, December 29th, 2019
49ers win, 26-21

The final month of the regular season began in the thick of the Gauntlet. The first leg of that rough stretch of games could not have gone better, with the Niners destroying Green Bay, 37-8, in the last game of a full-month home stand.

Leg two would not be nearly so easy, on the road and facing the NFL's hottest team, Baltimore. (The Ravens had won seven straight games.)

Week 13. Baltimore Ravens

As if this road game wasn't going to be tough enough, the weather was terrible, similar to the October 20th mudfest in Washington's pouring rain. But Washington sucked, and the Ravens most certainly did not suck.

They boasted the NFL's Most Valuable Player for 2019 at quarterback, a mobile passer adept at the zone read (read option) play. San Francisco countered that with the well-worn remedy of the scrape exchange, which Lamar Jackson exploited to pick up over 100 yards rushing. [74]

It's not that Niners defense had a bad day. Lamar Jackson had -- wait for it -- one of his worst games of the year, just 105 yards on 14 for 23 passing and a fumble.

Deebo Samuel scored another touchdown as San Francisco's receiving corps finally jelled into Kittle plus Sanders, Bourne and Samuel. That group would power the offense for the rest of the season, as Dante Pettis disappeared from the rotation and Marquise Goodwin hadn't played since the first Arizona game due to chronic injuries. (The team put him on the IR list December 10th.)

The bigger offensive story for San Francisco though was running back Raheem Mostert. Matt Breida hadn't played since the Seattle game, due in part to an ankle injury, and Mostert made the most of his opportunity with 146 yards and a touchdown against a tough defense.

In the end, it came down to kicking again. Robbie Gould was back from his injury and tied the game at 17 with a field goal near the end of the 3rd quarter. He had missed a 51-yarder at the end of the first half, though.

Justin Tucker won the game with a 49 yard field goal on the game's last play, after Jackson sustained a final drive for 6 and a half minutes.

Two more terrible injuries hit the SF defense: run-plugging nose tackle D.J. Jones, lost for the season, and safety Jaquiski Tartt, a serious rib injury that cost him several games. Both were quiet keys for the defense, and this was very worrisome heading toward the playoffs.

Week 14. New Orleans Saints

The gauntlet concluded on the road in New Orleans, a tough dome to play in. If anyone had residual doubts about Jimmy Garoppolo's ability to air it out and win a game with his arm, they were answered after this shootout.

Garoppolo threw it 35 times and the Nines won a thriller, 48-46. Both teams tried trick plays, and you could argue that San Francisco's success with theirs was the difference in the game.

New Orleans coach Sean Payton called a fake punt with gadget quarterback Taysom Hill throwing down the sideline to WR Tre-Quan Smith. It was a perfect pass, but DB Tarvarius Moore openly interfered with Smith's reception -- which was perfectly legal.

Saints fans howled, and perhaps Payton didn't know this, but pass interference is allowed on passes to the outside-most person on the line during fake punts. (Otherwise, punt reception units would be afraid to block the gunner.)

Presumably if Payton knew this, he'd just have had Smith line up inside a special teams gunner. Chalk one up for Moore knowing the rulebook better than a veteran coach.

San Francisco's trickery was more effective. Emmanuel Sanders took a pitch on a reverse, then threw deep to Raheem Mostert, who had slipped out on a wheel route as the flashy run play monopolized the defense's attention. Touchdown, 49ers.

It boiled down to two great quarterbacks dueling to win the game. Drew Brees led a drive for the go-ahead touchdown to Smith with 53 seconds left.

Garoppolo answered, hitting Kittle on 4th down for a short 7-yard out with some yards after the catch -- 31 of them to be exact, even as DB Marcus Williams openly yanked on the tight end's facemask as hard as he could. So add 15 more yards on the penalty.

Robbie Gould hit a 30 yard field goal as time expired for the win.

The three feared games against top opponents were over, and San Francisco had won two of them. It turned out the Niners were the gauntlet, after all.

Week 15. Atlanta

After surviving -- and thriving -- despite massive injuries against elite NFL competition, the Niners were ripe for a letdown against the 4-9 Falcons, and Atlanta plucked them.

The Falcons knew Kyle Shanahan's offense very well, of course, considering that they practiced against it all year in 2015 and 2016. According to scheme analyst Ted Nguyen,

> *"It looked like the 49ers weren't ready for how varied the Falcons were with their coverages. They played Cover 3, Tampa 2, Cover 6 and other forms of man coverage and they did a good job of disguising it, which seemed to cause Jimmy Garoppolo to hesitate at times."* [75]

The secondary was deeply depleted with CB Richard Sherman, strong safety Jaquiski Tartt and slot corner K'Waun Williams all out. That's not what you want against Matt Ryan and Julio Jones, and the pair made San Francisco pay with a winning touchdown that came with two ticks on the clock.

The upshot was that, even at 11-3, the Niners needed to win both of their final games to clinch the #1 seed in the NFC West and earn a week of rest to heal up all of their injuries.

And they would have beat their rival Seattle, who had already beaten them, in Seattle just to win their division and get even a single week of home field advantage under all but the most unlikely scenarios. Division winners are automatically seeded ahead of wild card teams in the playoffs, even if they have a losing record as Seattle did in the 2010 season.

Week 16. Los Angeles Rams

Los Angeles did not have a good year in 2019, entering their late season matchup with San Francisco 8-6. For all the praise of QB Jared Goff and coach Sean McVay, they weren't doing much better than all of those 8-8 Jeff Fisher teams.

But they're certainly not a team to be ignored, especially not a week after San Francisco let Atlanta sneak up on them.

San Francisco was dispirited, too, after learning earlier in the day that backup quarterback C. J. Beathard's brother had been killed outside a bar in Tennessee.

The late-season pattern continued for the 49ers: their hobbled defense allowed more points, especially in the first half, leading to a shootout and the QBs dueling with last second drives for the win (or not).

San Francisco played to stop the Rams' run game but left themselves vulnerable to bootlegs, and Goff killed them on these in the first half (8-8, 96 yards, one touchdown.)

Once again, Saleh adjusted, as Ted Nguyen recounts, reducing LA's bootleg production to 2-8, 24 yards after the break.

> *"In the second half, Saleh's adjustment was to have the 49ers ends play contain rather than play inside gaps. The simple adjustment worked to near perfection, as the 49ers held Goff to an average of 3 yards per pass attempt on boots in the second half."*
> 76

In the end it boiled down to another last-second drive for all the marbles, after the Rams' kicker Greg Zuerlein tied the game at 30 with 2:30 left.

Starting at his own 25, Garoppolo was sacked twice on the drive and had to convert two different 3rd-and-16s -- which he did. Kendrick Bourne picked up 18 up the middle on the first, and the second went to Emmanuel Sanders for 46.

Robbie Gould kicked a 33-yarder as time ran out. Now the division crown -- and #1 seed in the playoffs -- depended entirely on the showdown with Seattle. In Seattle.

Week 17. Seattle Seahawks

-- Akash Anavarathan

The Seahawks had handed the 49ers their first loss of the season, in Levi's Stadium no less. A second loss to Seattle on the road would make the 49ers' path to a seventh Super Bowl appearance infinitely more difficult.

There were only two possible outcomes. A win in Seattle would cement their status as the No. 1 seed – playing every game at home – while a loss would leave them 12-4 and the No. 5 seed,
behind their 9-7 opponent, Philadelphia.

While San Francisco was the healthier, more complete team, the horrors that Century Link Field presented could not be understated. Wilson had never lost to the 49ers there, though this would be the most talented 49ers' team he had faced during his run as Seattle's starting signal caller.

To add to the nostalgia of the Seahawks-49ers' rivalry from the early 2010s, Seattle signed running back Marshawn Lynch early in the week, after injuries knocked out tailbacks Chris Carson and C.J. Prosise.

Seattle was also without tackle Duane Brown and safety Quandre Diggs, which helped. Then again, let's not forget that San Francisco had 15 players on the Injured Reserve list.

A strong first half

Shanahan could not have asked for a better start from his team, as the 49ers opened up a 13-0 advantage in the first half and looked to be cruising to an NFC West title.

At halftime, I got a text from one of my friends who lives in the Pacific Northwest, "It's over. Looks like a Varsity-JV game." I had seen too many Wilson-Carroll games to ever be confident that the game was in control before the clock struck zero. But I take no joy in telling you that I was right.

The beauty of the Seahawks-49ers' rivalry is that it's like a heavyweight fight – both teams can take big punches and deliver striking blows. Neither team is going to tap out, and fans know they'll get four quarters of high-level entertainment.

Body blow! Body blow! As they continued to trade touchdowns, 49ers' running back Raheem Mostert danced into the end zone with 5:55 remaining in the fourth quarter to put San Francisco up 26-14.

My phone buzzed once again from the same friend and this time it read "It's over." I wrote back "Hold on, not yet." Like every 49ers fan, I had seen this movie before. Like every 49ers fan, I hate this movie.

Body blow! 26-21. Wilson's late-game heroics were on full display, and San Francisco's defense was reeling without pass rusher Dee Ford and linebacker Kwon Alexander (both were out injured). Robert Saleh's unit had played a lot of second-half snaps and were falling prey to quick throws from Wilson to his rag-tag bunch of receivers.

The 49ers stalled, and as punter Mitch Wishnowsky returned the ball to Ciara's husband, I lost hope in the ability of the 49ers' defense to take a stand against one of the most clutch quarterbacks in the NFL.

I started to scour the internet for flights to Philadelphia and shot a text to my dad, who was watching the game in California, giving him my best Bill Belichick impression: "The game is over. On to Philadelphia."

With 2:27 remaining, the Seahawks' offense had the ball on their own 27-yard line, down five points and poised to steal the souls of 49ers fans one more time.

We all knew this was coming. The NFL knew it too, which is why they scheduled these teams against each other in week 17. As the year went on, it became abundantly clear that the NFC West title was going to come down to that final game in Seattle.

After months of offseason workouts, training camp, preseason, 16 regular season games and 57 minutes in the finale, the 49ers' season was going to rest in the murderous hands of their arch nemesis – Russell Wilson.

Time and time again, I've watched the Seahawks' quarterback lead his offense down the field in the waning moments of a game and drag them past the finish line – especially in front of the raucous Century Link crowd.

Sure enough, Seattle marches right down the field: 5 yards, 10 yards, incomplete; 11 yards, 24 yards, incomplete, and 11 more. Suddenly they have a first down on the 12-yard line with 55 seconds left, and the NFC West crown is slipping away from the 49ers' grasp. Shanahan stands calmly on the sideline, looking helpless as the defense bends to Wilson's will.

While the next eight plays consume only 43 seconds of game time, it feels like an eternity. The tension is incredible, but San Francisco's defense is not breaking. Three straight nerve-wracking incompletions and Seattle is facing a fourth-and-10. True desperation time, and this time the desperation is theirs.

With their season on the line, Wilson hits John Ursua – another no-name receiver – for a 11-yard gain and a first down at the one yard line. Now, the momentum has swung back Seattle's way. They have four cracks at the end zone with a chance to ruin their resurgent rival's successful season and celebrate an NFC West title over an arch enemy in front of their ecstatic hometown fans.

Marshawn Lynch is trotting out to the field for the inevitable. The same player that tortured the 49ers in the early 2010s is about to leap over the goal line and into the north end zone, capping off a game-winning drive and sending the 49ers down to the Wild Card game.

Then, two key plays that will be forgotten in future years, but loom large in the story of this matchup.

First, Seattle rushes up to the line with 23 seconds left and Russell Wilson decides to stop the clock by spiking the ball, as soon as the ball is placed on the half-yard line. Rather than pushing through with their momentum and having Lynch pound it home, they stop to think and give San Francisco time to set up their formidable short-yard defense. It's also second down now, instead of first.

Then, as the Seahawks are making their offensive substitutions, they somehow lose track of the play clock, which hits zero before they are even lined up. Five-yard penalty for delay of game, and now it's 2nd-and-6, with no benefit to Seattle. The situation goes from a Lynch leap to a passing play, and the 49ers reset their defense once more.

An incompletion. Another incompletion, and now it is fourth-and-goal (remember the spike?). Seattle needs six yards to win all the marbles. Wilson drops back and finds tight end Jacob Hollister, who's met immediately by 49ers' rookie Dre Greenlaw and tackled right around the goal line.

On the goal line? Over it? No, just in front of it, about six inches shy.

It looks like the 49ers have clinched the No. 1 seed by protecting every last blade of grass and holding Hollister back from rolling over into the end zone.

Greenlaw remembered from the first game that Russell Wilson likes Hollister in the red zone, and he was ready to stop him.

Chaos ensues at the end of the play, as the ball is jarred loose and 49ers' safety Jimmie Ward scoops it up, running it back all the way to the far end zone as San Francisco's players are celebrating on the field.

The normally boisterous Seattle crowd goes quiet as they try to figure out whether Hollister broke the plane of the end zone, watching endless replays on the jumbotron while the zebras do the same on their tiny TVs. Head referee Tony Corrente finally announces that the Seahawks' tight end is indeed short and that the 49ers are going to take over on downs, sending the visitor's sideline into mayhem.

Then John Lynch embraced Kyle Shanahan – their three-year effort to rebuild a disastrous 49ers' franchise was finally coming to fruition. Veteran Joe Staley rejoiced at his chance to go back to the playoffs in his final years, and team captain Richard Sherman quietly enjoyed the fact that he was able to overcome all the naysayers and demolish his former team on the way to a Super Bowl appearance.

San Francisco had prepared for this very moment eight months ago, when they spent their fifth-round pick on the Arkansas linebacker, adding to a group that featured Fred Warner and recently-signed Kwon Alexander. Greenlaw was not going to start in the most common (nickel) package, but he would play on base downs and develop experience alongside Warner and Alexander.

Then Alexander went down with a torn pectoral muscle, and Greenlaw played a big part in replacing him. From his first game it was obvious that he was a technically-sound playmaker.

For the rookie to make that play in that moment will forever live in 49ers' lore, ranking with another goal-line stop by another number 57 -- Dan Bunz – that cemented San Francisco's first Super Bowl victory.

The 49ers were not satisfied with their first win in Seattle since 2011, or their second divisional title in this decade; they were out for a sixth Lombardi Trophy back to 4949 Marie P. DeBartolo Way.

Kyle Shanahan said it best without speaking at all. He just held up the celebratory t-shirt that read "The West Is Not Enough." The team was still two wins away from a Super Bowl appearance in Miami, and they still had work to do.

Chapter 8. Playoffs (Divisional Round)

Minnesota Vikings at San Francisco 49ers
January 11th, 2020
49ers win, 27-10

Getting the bye week during round one of the playoffs (the Wild Card Round) was crucial as the 49ers worked to get everyone healthy again.

The team's early bye in week 4 meant players had been grinding continuously for 3 months, as long as any NFL team ever does to end a season.

Emmanuel Sanders had it even worse -- since he was traded before Denver's bye week, he played 17 straight games without a rest.

The extra week also gave the coaching staff an extra week to catch their breath and take stock of the situation.

When San Francisco first hired him as coach, Kyle Shanahan had made it clear that he wanted to sign Kirk Cousins as a free agent, before Jimmy Garoppolo fell into his lap. (Washington had drafted Cousins as a backup to RGIII when Shanahan was their offensive coordinator in 2012-2013.)

By the time his first playoff game as head coach rolled around, he must have been glad he didn't.

Cousins has earned a reputation as a hot-and-cold QB who builds up his statistics against losing teams and fades under the spotlight, or against stern defenses. And he did nothing to disprove that image against San Francisco. The return of Dee Ford, Jaquiski Tartt and Kwon Alexander did not make Cousins' job any easier. He ended up 21 for 29 for 172 yards, but he gave back 46 of those yards on six sacks.

Cousins' 41-yard touchdown pass to Stefon Diggs in the first quarter was his only highlight of the game. Ahkello Witherspoon was the defender, continuing his late season slide (giving up five touchdowns in just three games: the last two games of the regular season and this one).

Not surprisingly, Robert Saleh benched Witherspoon for Emmanuel Moseley, and Minnesota's offense sputtered during the remaining three quarters. Notably they were 0 for 10 on third and fourth down attempts; it's hard to win a playoff game that way.

Cousins was 5 of 7 for 65 yards (13 yards per pass attempt) and a touchdown with Witherspoon in the game, compared to 16 of 22 for 102 yards (4.6 YPA) and an interception while facing Moseley.

Dalvin Cook, who had 98 yards and 2 touchdowns in the Vikings' upset victory over New Orleans, managed just 18 against San Francisco (on 9 carries) as Minnesota totaled 21 yards on the ground.

Minnesota went three-and-out on their first drive, followed by a San Francisco touchdown. The Vikings offense stalled over and over, going for almost half an hour of game time (starting in the second quarter) without a first down. Their 147 total yards was the fewest the 49ers have ever allowed during their long and very successful playoff history.

San Francisco put the game away for good in the third quarter. Richard Sherman intercepted Cousins on Minnesota's first drive of the second half, stepping in front of Adam Thielen. Then the Niners scored on eight straight runs that burned nearly five minutes off the clock, padding the lead to 24-10.

San Francisco slowed it down and ground it out after that for a 27-10 victory, never seriously threatened.

Jimmy Garoppolo did not have impressive statistics (11 for 19, 131 yards, 1 TD, 1 INT) but he came through when it mattered. On the first playoff drive of his career, he was 5 for 6 for 57 yards, throwing to 4 different receivers to score the game's first points.

He gave up only two sacks for nine yards, and the Niners were 5 for 12 on third down (including a Garoppolo keeper for two yards that moved the chains).

With 1:49 left in the first quarter, for example, the 49ers faced a third-and-ten just short of midfield. In such an obvious passing situation, Minnesota's coach Mike Zimmer double-teamed George Kittle and Deebo Samuel, bracketing them (which was a big compliment to the rookie).[77]

Despite intense pressure, Garoppolo stood tall in the pocket and lofted the ball to a safe spot near the sideline, right before he got clobbered. Kendrick Bourne dove and caught it for a 16-yard gain and a first down at the Minnesota's 36-yard line. [78]

After deducting yardage lost on sacks, Cousins gained only 4 more yards passing than Garoppolo, despite throwing 10 more passes. San Francisco passed just 11 times, but still scored 27 points thanks to a couple of turnovers and their run game, which picked up 186 yards on 47 carries.

Tevin Coleman was the lead back with 105 yards, but Raheem Mostert added 58 more (averaging 4.8 yards per carry each) and Matt Breida chimed in with 17.

Does Garoppolo deserve any credit for the good run game? Absolutely. Beyond his skill at bootlegs and RPOs, which help hold the defense back, Garoppolo isn't afraid to block himself.

Early in the second quarter, he was the lead blocker on a Deebo Samuel reverse and pancaked Minnesota's 6'5", 255-pound linebacker Anthony Barr, who will probably never stop getting razzed about it by his teammates.

Afterwards, tackle Mike McGlinchey was impressed.

> *"That was awesome. I saw that out of the corner of my eye, and Jimmy put him on his ass. That's a pretty good play by him. Maybe we'll put him in at fullback at some point."* [79]

Garoppolo said

"It felt good. Just sometimes you have to remember you're not just a quarterback, you're a football player too sometimes. Just tried to do my job on it."
80

Return of Kwon
-- Kyle Breitkreutz

On December 14th, Kendrick Bourne posted a video on Instagram of Kwon Alexander practicing. The 49ers had two available "IR designated to return" spots, which led 49ers fans to believe that there was an outside chance that Kwon Alexander could make the impossible happen and return for the 2019 season.

Coach Shanahan initially shot down the idea, it would be a long-shot for Alexander to return for the post season. But there were unofficial murmurings that built hope.

On radio station 95.7 "The Game," WR Kendrick Bourne said that Kwon told him that he would return this season. Then, on January 5th, tip-monger Adam Schefter reported Kwon would be available for the divisional round against the Vikings.

Five days later, the 49ers activated the linebacker. Kyle Shanahan said that Alexander was ready, but his playing time would be a coach's decision.

Kwon told reporters that he had leaned on J.J. Watt, who suffered the same injury at about the same point in the season, and that they motivated each other to keep working towards a comeback. Both men were expected to miss the rest of the season; both came back in about two months.

Not every story has a fairy tale ending. Kwon did not win a post-season game with an interception or stone anybody just short of the goal line. He had just 3 tackles in the 3 playoff games.

But he really is the heart of the Niners' defense, and his return gave the team a huge psychological boost that helped lead them to the Super Bowl.

Chapter 9. NFC Championship Game

Green Bay Packers at San Francisco 49ers
January 18, 2020
49ers win, 37-20

Before the biggest game of his short head coaching career (up to that point), Kyle Shanahan had a story for his team. It wasn't pretty, or cute, or even really inspiring except in the harshest of ways.

As Albert Breer of the MMQB recounted it, [81] it was a story Shanahan heard from a Navy SEAL.

> *"The soldier was explaining combat, and he emphasized that finishing the job might mean drowning an enemy who was scratching and clawing and fighting for his life. It meant, in the soldier's words, beating back all resistance, and holding his head under water until "the last bubble" was gone...."*

This was an analogy about the Packers. They had been severely wounded in their November game against the Niners game, but they were coming back to San Francisco, fighting desperately for their lives.

I wouldn't recommend repeating this anecdote at a cocktail party, but it hit home with the young warriors on his team.

> *"It was a little dark, but he got the message across,"* said tailback Raheem Mostert.

Tackle Mike McGlinchey was more effusive.

"I remember walking out of that meeting last night being like, 'Holy s---, I got the coolest coach of all-time. We're gonna win, there's no doubt about it.' That's what's cool about it. It was a mindset thing just to never relinquish what's going on in the football 49ers game, it was about how things are going to happen."

San Francisco had dominated the teams' first matchup, but all the pundits swore that this game would be different.

It wasn't, except that the Niners were even more dominant. They led at halftime 27-0, after a disastrous second quarter for Green Bay.

If it seemed like San Francisco ran a lot against Minnesota, they ran even more on the Packers. Raheem Mostert ran for 160 yards and 3 touchdowns -- in the first half.

San Francisco ended up passing only 8 times in the entire game. Why would they pass more, when Minnesota couldn't stop the run?

Mostert finished with 4 touchdowns and 220 yards, the second-most in NFL playoff history. (Only Eric Dickerson has ever topped that, with 248 yards for the Rams in January, 1986.)

Not bad for a surfer-skater dude cut by 6 NFL teams before he found a home in San Francisco.

Meanwhile, Robert Saleh's defense shut down Rodgers completely before the break. Here are the results of the Packers' first half drives:

Punt
Punt
Punt
Fumble (strip sack)
Interception
Punt

Aaron Rodgers did *not* have one of the worst games of his career this time -- he ended up 31-39 for 326 yards and 2 TDs -- but the first half was probably the worst half he ever had while completing 75% of his throws.

At halftime, he was 9 of 12 passing, but four of those completions gained under 3 yards. (Two of them lost yardage.)

The nine passes by Rodgers netted only 51 yards of offense, and he set San Francisco up for 17 easy points in a disastrous 10-minute stretch that ended the second quarter.

Already behind 10-0 on the road, Green Bay had 3 consecutive drives that ended badly, with
      1) a fumble they recovered, followed by a shanked 23-yard punt that gave San Francisco the ball at the Packers' 37,
      2) a lost fumble, and
      3) an interception.

San Francisco converted these opportunities into a touchdown, a field goal and another touchdown.

Davante Adams also had a statistically better game than in week 12, with 138 yards receiving on 11 targets (9 receptions), though half of those yards came on one 4th-quarter pass.

You knew that Green Bay would come back after halftime, and they did. The Packers scored touchdowns on their first three drives of the second half, and you could feel the tension wash over Levi's Stadium, which had been wild in the first half.

But the Niners kept scoring, responding to these drives with a touchdown, a punt and a field goal. San Francisco's lead was just too big, and all of this scoring had only cut the home team's lead to 17.

Green Bay got the ball back with 3:26 left in the game, trailing 37-20, and advanced no further than their own 38 yard line before Richard Sherman intercepted the ball to seal the game.

And San Francisco was in the Super Bowl again.

"A violent and physical team"

-- Mark Saltveit

There's no dispute that Kyle Shanahan calls a lot of clever plays and formations. But sometimes a team with that style gets a reputation as a "finesse team," which can be a code word for soft. Slight. Easy to push around. And maybe some of his early teams even deserved that label.

But going into 2019, it was clear that Shanahan wasn't having that any more. Maybe the success of George Kittle showed him the power of punishing defenders. Or maybe Shanahan realized that yards after the catch -- and yards on runs that get past the linebackers -- are a lot easier to pick up than those first five yards past the line of scrimmage.

Skill players who can just steamroll defenders simplify your game-planning a lot.

Most likely, this new toughness reflects the influence of General Manager John Lynch, who was a famously hard-hitting safety himself (with 4 All-Pro appearances in his 11 years as a player). That's certainly what George Kittle thinks.

> *"I think what we've done a good job at all year, offense, defense and special teams, is we have gone out there and we have hit people in the face. It starts with coach Shanahan and obviously it starts with John Lynch, how he talks about playing football, and we've seen plenty of his highlights, and stuff like*

that. It starts up there, and saying 'hey, we want to be a violent and physical team'." [82]

Whatever it was, the Niners made toughness, size and even brutality a priority during the off season. On a team that had drafted defensive linemen in the first round for three years out of the last four, Lynch went out and got two more: #2 overall pick Nick Bosa, and edge rusher Dee Ford.

He signed big, fast running back Tevin Coleman (6'1", 197 pounds while still running a 4.34 in the 40 yard dash.) And every single draft pick was a bruiser, including cornerback Tim Harris (6'2, 205") and Australian punter Mitch Wishnowsky (6'2", 220) who destroyed at least two returners with crunching open-field tackles for his new team.

Lynch's fifth round pick, linebacker Dre Greenlaw, was already a star by the end of his rookie season. Though small for a linebacker at 5'11" and 237 pounds, he bench-pressed 24 reps at the combine[83] and had no trouble stoning 6'4" Seattle TE Jacob Hollister at the goal line, in the single biggest play of the regular season.

A lot of teams have physical defenses, and the 49ers are no exception. But they have an unusually punishing *offense*, too, which is less common. Kittle:

> *"As an offense, we come off the ball and we hit people. Our wide receivers are cracking on safeties and corners and when your <u>wide receivers</u> are physical, you have a physical team."* [84]

Lynch's second and third round picks were both large, hard-hitting receivers who could easily run through defensive backs. Though he missed the season due to injury, Jalen Hurd is a former running back with tight end size (6'5" and 10 & 1/4" hands) who converted to wide receiver. He was a bit thin at 226 pounds, but there is no doubt the team will try to beef him up. Hurd is a prototype of Shanahan-style versatility, with a huge potential upside and the speed and size to create matchup problems all over the field.

But aside from the unstoppable Bosa (who you already know about), it was WR Deebo Samuel who best illustrated the advantages of muscle and a willingness to hit. He gained 802 yards receiving and another 159 on runs, and for the most part they were pretty simple plays with lots of yards after the catch. Deebo often just steamrolled defensive backs. Given how good a route runner he is, the rookie has a lot of untapped potential.

This became the team's unstated ethic. No one minded when the punter got an unnecessary roughness penalty for de-cleating a returner. As we've seen, even quarterback Jimmy Garoppolo knocked a linebacker to the ground while lead-blocking on a Deebo Samuel reverse.

The other side of the ball -- the one with five first round picks on the defensive line -- is not too wispy, either. George Kittle felt that in practice, playing against those guys.

"Our defense is an absolute monster. It is, from every single position, from K'Waun Williams to

Richard Sherman to Nick Bosa. There's a lot of guys out there that are going to take your head off. You know, Kwon Alexander, and Fred Warner.

I don't want to get hit by those guys. So, as an offense when you feel that, you're kind of like, you've got to bring it or else you're going to get hit pretty hard." [85]

By the week before the Super Bowl, Kittle was taking notes on which players had *not* flattened an opponent this year:

"It's a game changer. I think we've done a really good job all year of just putting physical [play] on tape. From every position. I mean, even Mitch! [Wishnowsky] Our kicker laid a guy out in a preseason game. We still give him [a hard time]. That's incredible. We're still waiting on [kicker] Robbie Gould to hit someone but we'll wait for it." [86]

Or maybe there *were* some other players who needed to hit more. Wide receivers were joining in the physicality all year, blocking hard and talking about how much they enjoyed it. Before the Super Bowl, Emmanuel Sanders said:

"Man. There ain't nothing like grabbing a dude, and you're blocking a dude, and I swear—this is the God's honest truth: It might be a better feeling than scoring a touchdown, seeing a running back running off your block into the end zone. Just one of the best feelings ever." [87]

One voice notably absent was that of Dante Pettis, the second-year receiver with a unique touchdown celebration that imitated a cat licking its paws. Speculation was that the passes he dropped in the loss to Seattle put him in the doghouse, so to speak, but it could also be that he didn't take to the blocking that Shanahan demands from receivers on run plays. Or that he simply didn't have the muscle to finish a block, even if he wanted to.

On a team where any given play could be a run or a pass, there is no room for receivers who won't block, or running backs who can't catch.

Heading into the Super Bowl, these players seemed to be sending a subtle message to the Chiefs that they were soft, and that San Francisco planned to bully them. No one would say that in so many words -- don't want to give anybody locker room cork-board material for motivation -- but the Chiefs are in fact a finesse team and the implication was there.

Nick Bosa -- who speaks more on the field than off -- put it simply.

> *"We take being physical very, very seriously," Bosa said. "A lot of teams are finesse in the NFL and I think you can expose them with physical play."* [88]

A lot of teams, or one team in particular? Either way, that sounded like a challenge to me.

Chapter 10. Super Bowl LIV

vs. Kansas City Chiefs
February 2nd, 2020
Miami Gardens, Florida

-- Akash Anavarathan

San Francisco charged into Super Bowl 54, winning their two home playoff games by a combined 34 points and leaving no doubt in fans' minds about who was the best team in the NFC.

Robert Saleh's defense had overcome every challenge during the season, limiting forcing several franchise quarterbacks into season-worst or even career-worst performances.

But the challenge that awaited them in the Super Bowl wasn't the hot-and-cold Vikings' offense or an underwhelming Aaron Rodgers' passing attack.

The Chiefs got to the big game behind MVP Patrick Mahomes, a plethora of speedy weapons on the outside and the NFL's second-best tight end all schemed up by two of the league's most creative offensive minds (Andy Reid and Eric Bieniemy).

On the flip side, the 49ers' offense had a slight advantage over the Chiefs' defense, as they had been the more consistent and talented unit all season long. But the team was very young, and QB Jimmy Garoppolo was going to need to throw a lot more than eight passes to win this battle.

The teams mirrored each other in a lot of ways. Both franchises are led by humble, offensive-minded head coaches that are well-regarded among their players. They have dominant tight ends as a pivotal part of their respective offenses, and prided themselves on being respectful and low-drama during the season. That was reflected in the lead-up to the Super Bowl. Outside of a few Frank Clark mouthings-off, there wasn't much trash talk or bulletin board material during the thousands of media sessions.

I couldn't think of another Super Bowl in recent memory that was more of a coin flip than this one. Kansas City closed as one-point favorites, so even the sports books assumed that it would be a close game, but they favored Mahomes in a tight contest.

San Francisco opened the game with their defensive unit on the field in front of a pro-Chiefs' crowd in Hard Rock stadium, forcing an immediate punt as Mahomes misfired with what looked like Super Bowl jitters.

Jimmy Garoppolo and Kyle Shanahan notched a field goal on the opening drive, as they were able to move the ball with ease – as expected against a weak Chiefs' run defense – but sputtered in the red zone.

The first half was headlined by faltering offensive play for two teams that were top-five scoring offenses during the regular season. The game's biggest controversy came at the end of the first half, when Kyle Shanahan let the clock run down without calling a time out during a drive in the last two minutes, as his team tried to add more points before the half.

Instead, Shanahan chose a conservative approach, taking his shot only after making sure there wasn't enough time left for Kansas City to drive before the half. Garoppolo then connected on a 20-yard pass to Jeff Wilson, Jr. and a 42-yard bomb to Kittle at the Kansas City 13 yard line, with 14 seconds left.

But Kittle's catch was taken away by a controversial offensive pass interference call, so San Francisco settled for a 10-10 tie going into the extra-long halftime session.

When asked about his decision making after the game, Shanahan said that he was "content" with his decision and did not want to give Andy Reid's offense another chance before the end of the second quarter.

In the moment, I was angered by his decision because the 49ers' offense had the Chiefs' defense on the ropes – outside of a Garoppolo interception – and taking the foot off the gas didn't seem to fit Shanahan's M.O. as an aggressive head coach.

San Francisco's motto during the regular season was "All Gas No Brakes," but in the season's most crucial moments, they lightly tapped the brakes to slowly cruise into the second half rather than accelerating past the Chiefs with either three or seven points on the final drive.

But in hindsight, Shanahan's plan worked perfectly, except for the penalty. He first made sure Kansas City couldn't score, then called a play that put the ball in chip-shot field goal range, with a chance at scoring a touchdown fist -- since the Niners had a time out left.

The third quarter was nearly perfect for San Francisco. They added 10 points, while intercepting Patrick Mahomes and holding the Chiefs scoreless. The 49ers had lost three games on the season, but not once did they lose when having a double-digit lead going into the final quarter.

On the Chiefs' first possession of the fourth quarter, the 49ers picked off Mahomes for his second turnover of the evening and I started to picture the confetti coming down on Kyle Shanahan and Jed York as Terry Bradshaw handed them the Lombardi Trophy.
I did not imagine the 49ers' defense giving up more than 10 points in the final 8:59 of the game, given the way that the defensive line had handled the Chiefs' quarterback during the game.

There were two moments in this game that I wish the 49ers could go back and change

It was third-and-15 with a little over seven minutes left and the Chiefs were desperate to get a first down to keep their drive – and season – alive. The 49ers are a solid tackling team and were not known to give up heavy yardage on third downs.

San Francisco decided to play Cover-3 on the back end and rush four up the middle – the 49ers' most-used defensive alignment in these situations.

They say football is a game of inches and the 49ers' defensive line was maybe a split second away from landing a sack on Mahomes that could have crippled Kansas City's chances of winning their first Super Bowl in over 50 years.

Instead, Mahomes narrowly escaped a sack and launched a 44-yard bomb to a wide-open Tyreek Hill who was waiting for the catch without a defender in the picture frame. All of a sudden, my heart sank to my stomach, as I could feel the Chiefs start to hit a rhythm on offense.

49ers' corner Emmanuel Moseley seemed to misplay the coverage and it turned into a bust, as Hill ran wide open through the teeth of San Francisco's defense. I wish we could reverse time and allow for Moseley to be in the right position to make a play. Yet, he wasn't and the Chiefs made them pay for it.

The Chiefs – especially Mahomes – reminded me of Stephen Curry and the 2016 Golden State Warriors.

During their 73-win season, the Warriors would often go many nights during the regular season where it felt like they were sleepwalking through the game. Yet, all of a sudden Curry would bury a three, followed by a Klay Thompson trey. All of a sudden, the flood gates would open and the avalanche was on.

The Chiefs' offense has that type of feel, where all it takes is one play to uncork their offense and get them back on track. On Sunday, that one play was the 44-yard pass play to Hill on third down and fifteen. Before I could blink, Mahomes was celebrating a touchdown pass to Travis Kelce and the 49ers' lead had dwindled to three points.

All I knew was that the 49ers could not punt the ball back to the Chiefs with six minutes left – if they couldn't score on this drive, they could effectively kiss the Lombardi Trophy good bye. Which leads to the second play the Niners would love to get back.

On the subsequent drive, the 49ers had the Chiefs' defense reeling after multiple first downs. On second-and-five, Shanahan had identified a matchup where George Kittle was lined up against Chiefs' Terrell Suggs and made him the primary read on the play.

Garoppolo snapped the ball and saw that Kittle was getting open against Suggs with a whole lot of green grass ahead of him if he catches the ball. Chiefs' defensive tackle Chris Jones had other plans, batting the ball down and forcing third down.

Instead of nabbing a first down near mid-field with 5:25 remaining, Garoppolo threw two straight incompletions and the 49ers were forced to punt to Mahomes, who was red-hot after the latest touchdown drive. That Steph Curry-like avalanche kept rolling for the Chiefs' offense.

After a 38-yard pass to Sammy Watkins, the Chiefs were cooking and on their way to putting up 21 unanswered points after it looked like they had no hope.

As Harrison Butker put the Chiefs up 24-20, I sat down and closed my eyes, thinking that a magical 13-3 49ers' team that earned fans across the country was going to fumble away a 10-point lead in the fourth quarter while chasing their first Super Bowl title in 25 years.

San Francisco's offense sputtered in the final frame, not putting up any points as Garoppolo finished the game with five straight incompletions and an interception while trying to will the 49ers to a win.

Kyle Shanahan ran off the field, watching as once again confetti rained down on another opponent who was able to come back from large deficit in the fourth quarter of the Super Bowl.

Nick Bosa was on the sideline sobbing, as the rookie couldn't deliver on a knockout blow in the final moments of the game, potentially altering the final result. Joe Staley was emotional during the post-game presser, realizing that his time in the NFL was dwindling and he might not get another opportunity to win a Super Bowl.

San Francisco was a well-oiled machine for 18.75 games, yet failed to execute on all levels in the last 15 minutes of their season and it cost them a championship.

Will they be back? It's tough to say. The foundation for the franchise is set in stone, but in a sport that features one-

and-out playoffs and a lot of variance from year-to-year, it's hard to predict what will happen 12 months from now.

But I won't bet against this legendary squad. After the game, George Kittle sat in the locker room next to Kwon Alexander and told him:

> *"Revenge tour, baby. The Legendary Revenge Tour of 2020. It's coming. And I can't f------ wait."*

Get ready for the Revenge Tour of 2020.

(Over)Confidence

-- Kyle Posey

The San Francisco 49ers appeared in Super Bowl LIV for numerous reasons, but one of the main factors was their confidence.

Well before the regular season started, many folks "inside the building" (i.e. 49ers staff) felt that this team could be special, that it would be as good as we eventually saw on the field during 2019.

That confidence bled into the players, and they started to speak it into existence. Kwon Alexander's energy was apparent from the first time he stepped on the field. Newcomers Dee Ford and Nick Bosa made an impact right away as well.

Adding good players is one thing. Adding good players that fit your teams' culture is a different story. Ironically, the teams' confidence ultimately did them in.

There was a video making its way (and making waves) around the internet after the 49ers lost. It showed cornerback Richard Sherman screaming, pleading for his teammates to stay focused and not to relax because "this sh-t ain't over!"

Rookie linebacker Dre Greenlaw responded, "Nah, we got this." The Chiefs scored a touchdown on their next three possessions and the rest is history that San Francisco wanted to avoid.

I was fortunate enough to attend Super Bowl week and all the hoopla that comes with it, as a reporter. The vibe I got from the team was that they "knew." They knew they were the better team. They knew they had the correct game plan to foil Andy Reid and the Chiefs. For three and a half quarters, the Niners had every reason to believe this. Even with hiccups--like an interception, or settling for field goals--the team still took a 10-point lead into the fourth quarter. You know how the rest turned out.

Rewind to the media festivities leading up to the game and the team made no secret that they were confident. I asked safety Jaquiski Tartt if he was tired of talking about how good the Chiefs were, to which Tartt responded,

> *"I love it. Y'all keep talking about 'em. They deserve it, so y'all keep talking about them. It makes it that much sweeter. It's lovely."*

That sentiment was consistent all week. All season, really.

Whenever you put a microphone in front of All-Pro cornerback Richard Sherman, he was quick to reference how well the entire defense played. A question about Sherman would turn into praising each member of the defense one by one.

That belief in each other--from the top down--is a big reason the team made it as far as they did. Raheem Mostert was nearly at a loss for words when I asked him what it means to have the overwhelming support of his teammates.

Unprovoked, Emmanuel Sanders said Mostert had the best chance to be MVP of Super Bowl LIV. Joe Staley and Mike McGlinchey would bring Mostert up as the hardest-working player on the team. Everyone works their butt off, but when you get recognized for it, it means something.

Think about your job. How often do you pick up the slack for someone else? How often does that work go unrecognized?
That wasn't the case in 2019 for the 49ers. When talking to each defensive linemen, to a man, they pointed to Dee Ford and his leadership. Really? A guy that played roughly 22% of the seasons' snaps had the biggest impact? Believe it.

Nick Bosa said Ford taught him how to finish. DeForest Buckner said Ford's speed opens up things for everyone. Arik Armstead praised his leadership, even though Ford was in his first season with the team. Armstead cited Ford's experience winning in the playoffs, as well as being extremely talented.

Ask anyone on the roster, and they'd find a way to praise someone else. Ask Deebo Samuel, and he'd talk about Emmanuel Sanders as if he'd given him the winning lottery ticket. The same goes for Kendrick Bourne. If overconfidence was part of the reason the 49ers came up short in the Super Bowl, that same bond and belief in each other will be the reason San Francisco makes it back to the big game sooner than later.

Chapter 11. The future

GM John Lynch and head coach Kyle Shanahan have built this team for the long haul, for continued success over a five or ten year run. For a dynasty, not a playoff run.

The emphasis on team play, good character and versatility are excellent pillars to support long run success, and Kyle Shanahan's versatile, unpredictable offense is not the kind that can be "solved" like the wildcat scheme was.

The Niners will need to make hard choices, though. Success raises players' pay rates, and some will go elsewhere in free agency, making real money and setting up their families for life.

Good for them. Careers are short, grab it while you can. Others (perhaps veterans such as Joe Staley or Robbie Gould) might decide to retire now, thinking they're unlikely to reach the Super Bowl again in the twilight years of their career.

But winning makes player acquisition easier, too. Veterans with good attitudes want to play on a winner, a team with a great culture and a high likelihood of going deep in the playoffs for a few years at least. Those who have already made some serious money may be willing to take a discount for that opportunity.

Others players may want to join the team as role players late in their career. Julio Jones will become a free agent in

2024, at age 34, and might be happy to end his career as a depth receiver with his former Atlanta coach Shanahan.

Coaching changes

Good teams lose coaches, too, as they get promoted to bigger roles on other teams. San Francisco was lucky not to lose defensive coordinator Robert Saleh, one of the leading candidates for head coaching positions.

Here too the team's success helped. A new head coach is usually part of a major rebuilding process, and those teams may not have wanted want to wait extra weeks for candidates who were planning a Super Bowl game.

Hopefully, it was that timing issue, and not ethnicity that cause Kansas City's offensive coordinator Eric Bieniemy and Saleh to get passed over, because it's hard to see how Minnesota OC Kevin Stefanski or 38-year old special teams coordinator Joe Judge are better qualified to be head coaches than Saleh or Bieniemy.

Then again, maybe not coaching the Cleveland Browns and New York Giants is its own reward.

San Francisco did lose defensive passing game coordinator and defensive backs coach Joe Woods, now Stefanski's defensive coordinator in Cleveland, and defensive line assistant Chris Kiffin who left with him.

Frankly, the Niners were lucky to ever get Woods in the first place. It's tempting to speculate that he had been promised Saleh's job as the Niners' DC in case Saleh got a head coaching job somewhere.

The team hired Miami's defensive backs coach Tony Oden to replace Woods. He coached alongside DL coach Kris Kocurek in both Detroit and Miami, and did well coaching up young cornerbacks and generating interceptions -- perfect skills for this young team.

Hard choices

Any time you get a lot of great players as undrafted rookies or late draft picks, you are going to have to pay them a lot more on their second contracts. George Kittle will undoubtedly get the largest tight end contract ever, when his rookie deal expires in a year. Emmanuel Mosely, Kendrick Bourne, Ben Garland and Matt Breida are just four of the great free agent finds who will need to get paid if the team wants to keep them. Clearly, the 49ers can't afford to keep everyone.

History tells us, though, that investing in the defensive line is a shrewd strategy. The Philadelphia Eagles won their first Super Bowl in 2017, not because of their quarterback -- Carson Wentz was out injured -- or their skill players, who were mediocre at best.

It was their crushing defensive line that got them through the playoffs, right up through Brandon Graham's strip sack of Tom Brady to seal the game. And when the team let their DL decline, the team's fortunes declined too.

This suggests that, even though he'll be expensive, DL Arik Armstead is worth spending for, as is Dee Ford (if the team is comfortable that he can stay healthy.)

Adding to the Roster

The 49ers don't have many draft picks, due to trades. What do they need? A healthier edge rusher to replace Dee Ford would be the most valuable addition, but those players are hard to come by, and expensive when you can. It's unlikely the Niners will find a great one at the end of the first round.

Ahkello Witherspoon is too up-and-down to count on at cornerback any time soon, and a good second-tier cornerback could be available for their first round pick. An offensive tackle who might eventually start after Joe Staley retires would be nice, though the strength of Brunskill might encourage the team to take a more speculative or raw prospect on day three of the draft.

The best value given the Niners' low draft position, though, might be to build on a position of strength: tight end. Think back to the classic Patriots' lineups with Aaron Hernandez and Rob Gronkowski, and imagine what a second TE happy to block and adept at receiving could do in this offensive scheme. Top tight end prospects are usually available on day two of the draft; Zach Ertz was a round two pick, and Travis Kelce went in round three.

The strength of this team, already, is that defenses can't tell if they'll run or pass. A formation with fullback Juszczyk, two great tight ends, Deebo Samuel at wide receiver and

Tevin Coleman at running back would bring a ton of muscle -- and could quickly motion to an empty backfield for a spread offense passing concept. Players like Adam Trautman of Dayton or Albert Okwuegbunam of Missouri who have NFL size, athleticism and untapped potential both as blockers and receivers might be available at a reasonable price.

Returning players

Let's not forget the positive side of the 49ers rash of injuries; a lot of talent was lost for the rest of the season in 2019, and most of those guys will be back in 2020. That includes Swiss Army Knife Jalen Hurd, a WR/RB/TE who can build on this team's unique mix of physicality and speed, as well as center Weston Richburg, nose tackle DJ Jones, cornerback Tim Harris, slot receiver Trent Taylor, and pass rusher Ronald Blair III. So this team can improve a great deal just by healing up.

More generally, the emphasis on speed, physicality and versatility has given them the ability to keep winning, despite multiple key injuries, against grinding defenses or high-powered offenses, in rain-soaked slogfests or sunny September shootouts.

Continuing the legacy

Beyond the roster and scheme maneuvers, there is something bigger involved with this franchise. The San Francisco 49ers have a unique legacy of power, grace, intelligence and character over the last forty years. And both Lynch and Shanahan cut their teeth in that tradition.

Kyle Shanahan was a ball boy for the 49ers in their glory years, when his father, longtime coach Mike Shanahan, was the offensive coordinator under George Seifert, Bill Walsh's successor.

The elder Shanahan emulated Walsh's techniques including scripting his first 15 plays, and devised a run-heavy version of the West Coast Offense. John Lynch played for Walsh himself during his senior year at Stanford, and started at Tampa Bay under Sam Wyche, another member of the Walsh coaching tree.

The hallmark of the 1980s-90s 49ers was not just winning, but sustained winning, through different coaches, quarterbacks and entire generations of players. And that is the what this regime has aimed for. Not the sugar-rush, mortgage-the-future strategy that got the Los Angeles Rams to a single Super Bowl, where they were humiliated. As John Lynch said,

"We built it the right way, and the coolest thing is this is sustainable." [89]

The last decade has seen some dark and ugly times for the franchise, not so much just losing games as a loss of character -- years of back-stabbing in the front office, leaks to reporters criticizing coaches, players and team officials.

Those dark days are over now. Owner Jed York has grown immeasurably on the job, despite his young age, and seems to have found the right balance between getting involved and letting the men he hired do their job, between the desire to win and pride in winning the right way. Looking back on how this rebuilding process came together so suddenly in 2019, he saw the bigger picture:

> *"When we hit our stride from a talent standpoint, we had the culture in place."* [90]

The leaks have stopped, and the coach and general manager are working together closely, communicating forthrightly, and winning. They understand the legacy of this franchise, and are doing everything they can to rebuild that legacy.

This is 49ers football -- a team that you can be proud of not because they win, but because of *how* they win.

Contributors

Eric Crocker is a former pro cornerback who appears on the Better Rivals podcast and other podcasts, and writes for several football websites.

Mark Saltveit is an author and comedian based in Portland, Oregon. He has written for Niners Nation since 2016 and is the author of "The Tao of Chip Kelly" (2013) and "Controlled Chaos" (2015), both published by Diversion Books of New York. He also writes on Daoism (his blog is Taoish.org) and the history of palindromes, going back to Hellenistic Alexandria, Egypt (around 300 BCE).

Kyle Posey is the editor of Niners Nation.

Akash Anavarathan covers the 49ers for Vox Media's Niners Nation. He grew up in the Bay Area, following the 49ers intently since the Mike Singletary days. Now based in Seattle, he's an Electrical Engineer designing circuit boards by day.

Kyle Breitkreutz is a Bay Area sportswriter, and the manager and director of @49ersNoir, which produces the 49ersNoir podcast.

Alex Tran is a writer and social media specialist for Niners Nation.

References

[1] The Football Database (https://www.footballdb.com/stats/qb-records.html?type=&alltime=&sort=pct).
I'm ignoring Drew Lock (who has a 4-1 lifetime record) because, come on.

[2] Nick Wagoner, Twitter, January 15, 2020 (https://twitter.com/nwagoner/status/1217498964163022850)

[3] Josh Dubow, Twitter, January 15, 2020 (https://twitter.com/JoshDubowAP/status/1217504410563035136)

[4] Taylor Wirth, Twitter, January 31, 2020 (https://twitter.com/WirthTM/status/1223355906542358528)

[5] David Lombardi, "A decade of Richard Sherman: Back in the Super Bowl, the 49ers' star reminisces about a full-circle journey," The Athletic, January 27, 2020 (https://theathletic.com/1562357/2020/01/27/a-decade-of-richard-sherman-back-in-the-super-bowl-the-49ers-star-reminisces-about-a-full-circle-journey/)

[6] ibid

[7] Robert Saleh press conference, January 23, 2020

[8] Winston Chung (@dubcmd), January 24, 2020 (https://twitter.com/dubcmd/status/1220764449964838912)

[9] NinersNation official account, Twitter, January 30, 2020 (https://twitter.com/NinersNation/status/1223008031350444034)

[10] Cam Inman, Twitter, January 24, 2020 (https://twitter.com/CamInman/status/1220862671659995138)

[11] Football Outsiders Team Defense Rankings for 2019 (https://www.footballoutsiders.com/stats/nfl/team-defense/2019); Solomon Wilcots, "PFF Rankings: All 32 NFL coverage defenses through 17 weeks of the regular season," Pro Football Focus, January 13, 2020 (https://www.pff.com/news/nfl-2019-nfl-secondary-rankings)

[12] Chris Biderman, "49ers notebook: Teammates react to 'MVP' Kwon Alexander's return to practice," Sacramento Bee, January 2, 2020

(https://www.sacbee.com/sports/nfl/san-francisco-49ers/article238920063.html)

[13] (https://www.instagram.com/p/B4f_7OpDSYU/)

[14] Matt Maiocco, "49ers' Kwon Alexander feeling 'legendary' in his return from ACL injury," NBC Sports, July 29, 2019 (https://www.nbcsports.com/bayarea/49ers/49ers-kwon-alexander-feeling-legendary-his-return-acl-injury)

[15] Steven Ruiz, on Twitter, January 25, 2020 (https://twitter.com/thestevenruiz/status/1221207297621360640)

[16] Ted Nguyen, "Super Bowl analysis: Evaluating the 49ers offense vs. the Chiefs defense," The Athletic, January 23, 20120, (https://theathletic.com/1553550/2020/01/23/super-bowl-analysis-evaluating-the-49ers-offense-vs-the-chiefs-defense/)

[17] (https://twitter.com/NFL/status/1181365119990714368)

[18] Ben Linsey, "How Kyle Shanahan has taken the 49ers offense to the top of the NFL," Pro Football Focus, December 12, 2019 (https://www.pff.com/news/nfl-how-kyle-shanahan-has-taken-the-49ers-offense-to-the-top-of-the-nfl)

[19] Touchdowns 1, 2 & 5 in Ted Nguyen's article "49ers Film Room: Kyle Shanahan added some razzle-dazzle in his explosive game plan against the Saints," The Athletic, December 10, 2019 (https://theathletic.com/1444045/2019/12/10/49ers-film-room-kyle-shanahan-added-some-razzle-dazzle-in-his-explosive-game-plan-against-the-saints/)

[20] Oscar Aparicio and Eric Crocker, Better Rivals podcast, October 29, 2019 (https://www.ninersnation.com/2019/10/29/20939498/better-rivals-49ers-podcast-carolina-panthers-review-thursday-game-preview-arizona-cardinals)

[21] "NFL Films Presents: The Vanishing Fullback," YouTube, October 7, 2019 https://www.youtube.com/watch?v=VzNUoEXjxQ8&feature=youtu.be&t=122

[22] "Kyle Juszczyk flips pitch to Breida on slick triple option play," NFL Big Game Highlights, September 23, 2018

(http://www.nfl.com/videos/nfl-game-highlights/0ap3000000965512/Kyle-Juszczyk-flips-pitch-to-Breida-on-slick-triple-option-play)

[23] Ted Nguyen, "49ers Film Room: Kyle Juszczyk breaks down his favorite plays from last season", The Athletic, July 5, 2019 (https://theathletic.com/1059497/2019/07/05/49ers-film-room-kyle-juszczyk-breaks-down-his-favorite-plays-from-last-season/)

[24] ibid.

[25] Ted Nguyen, "49ers Film Room: Kyle Shanahan added some razzle-dazzle in his explosive game plan against the Saints," The Athletic, December 10, 2019 (https://theathletic.com/1444045/2019/12/10/49ers-film-room-kyle-shanahan-added-some-razzle-dazzle-in-his-explosive-game-plan-against-the-saints/)

[26] Ted Nguyen, "49ers Film Room: Robert Saleh's revamped scheme and pass rush came through in pivotal moments," The Athletic, September 11, 2019 (https://theathletic.co.uk/1201998/2019/09/11/49ers-film-room-robert-salehs-revamped-scheme-and-pass-rush-came-through-in-pivotal-moments/)

[27] ibid

[28] Ted Nguyen, "49ers vs. Packers preview: Green Bay will need a game for the ages from Aaron Rodgers to beat this defense", The Athletic, January 16, 2020 (https://theathletic.com/1538535/2020/01/16/49ers-vs-packers-preview-green-bay-will-need-a-game-for-the-ages-from-aaron-rodgers-to-beat-this-defense/)

[29] Jim Buzinski, "San Francisco 49ers assistant Katie Sowers is first out LGBT coach in NFL," Outsports.com, August 22, 2017 (https://www.outsports.com/2017/8/22/16175286/katie-sowers-san-francisco-49ers-coach-gay-coming-out)

[30] ibid

[31] David Lombardi, "A decade of Richard Sherman: Back in the Super Bowl, the 49ers' star reminisces about a full-circle journey," The Athletic, January 27, 2020 (https://theathletic.com/1562357/2020/01/27/a-decade-of-richard-sherman-back-in-the-super-bowl-the-49ers-star-reminisces-about-a-full-circle-journey/)

[32] Jed York press conference, quoted in the Paradise Post, January 24, 2020, (https://www.paradisepost.com/2020/01/24/49ers-owner-jed-york-super-bowl-liv-niners-white-house-visit-kyle-shanahan-john-lynch/)

[33] "49ers release Reuben Foster after domestic-violence arrest in Florida," by Eric Branch, San Francisco Chronicle, December 3, 2018 (https://www.sfchronicle.com/49ers/amp/49ers-Reuben-Foster-arrested-on-domestic-13419289.php)

[34] Keiana Martin, "Fast and Furious: How Speedy Are the 49ers Running Backs?", 49ers.com, May 17, 2018 (https://www.49ers.com/news/fast-and-furious-how-speedy-are-the-49ers-running-backs)

[35] Albert Breer, the MMQB, January 20, 2020 (https://www.si.com/nfl/2020/01/20/nfl-playoffs-super-bowl-liv-49ers-chiefs-patrick-mahomes-kyle-shanahan-mmqb)

[36] Chris Biderman, "Game Wrap: 49ers losing streak sets new mark in NFL history," USA Today: Niners Wire, October 15, 2017 (https://ninerswire.usatoday.com/2017/10/15/game-wrap-49ers-losing-streak-sets-new-mark-in-nfl-history/)

[37] -- Mark Saltveit, "The 'Elegant Tank' Rolls On," Niners Nation, October 20, 2017 (https://www.ninersnation.com/2017/10/20/16505240/49ers-tanking-kyle-shanahan-cj-beathard/comment/448853165);
-- Mark Saltveit, "Deeper into the 49ers Elegant Tank," Niners Nation, November 16, 2017 (https://www.ninersnation.com/2017/11/16/16666980/deeper-into-the-elegant-tank-beathard-garoppolo-kyle-shanahan/comment/452725669);
-- Oscar Aparicio (aka @BetterRivals), Twitter, December 16, 2018 (https://twitter.com/BetterRivals/status/1074445000581279745)

[38] "Police: Jets' Robinson had THC-laced candy," Bergen (New Jersey) Record, January 9, 2018 (https://www.northjersey.com/story/sports/nfl/jets/2018/01/09/report-new-york-jets-rashard-robinson-arrested-possession-thc-infused-candy-drug-marijuana/1019080001/)

[39] Daniel Mano, "The awesome way John Lynch reportedly tried to trade for Tom Brady," San Jose Mercury News, November 5, 2017"

(https://www.mercurynews.com/2017/11/05/how-john-lynch-reportedly-tried-to-trade-for-tom-brady/)

[40] Timothy Rapp, "Report: John Lynch Tried to Trade for Tom Brady While Pursuing Jimmy Garoppolo," Bleacher Report, November 5, 2019 (https://bleacherreport.com/articles/2742627-report-john-lynch-tried-to-trade-for-tom-brady-while-pursuing-jimmy-garoppolo)

[41] David Lombardi, "A decade of Richard Sherman: Back in the Super Bowl, the 49ers' star reminisces about a full-circle journey," The Athletic, January 27, 2020 (https://theathletic.com/1562357/2020/01/27/a-decade-of-richard-sherman-back-in-the-super-bowl-the-49ers-star-reminisces-about-a-full-circle-journey/)

[42] See Dieter Kurtenback, "Why a two-way player with a second job could be key to 49ers' playoff hopes," San Jose Mercury News, December 13, 2019 (https://www.mercurynews.com/2019/12/13/kurtenbach-why-new-49ers-center-ben-garland-is-oh-so-easy-to-root-for/)

[43] Kyle Posey, "PFF grades and snap counts from the 49ers blowout win over the Vikings," Niners Nation, January 13, 2020 (https://www.ninersnation.com/2020/1/13/21063151/pff-grades-and-snap-counts-from-the-49ers-blowout-win-over-the-vikings)

[44] Vincent Frank, "Breaking Down The 49ers' Blockbuster Trade For Emmanuel Sanders," Forbes Magazine, October 23, 2019 (https://www.forbes.com/sites/vincentfrank/2019/10/23/breaking-down-the-49ers-blockbuster-trade-for-emmanuel-sanders/#12c6206a2f3e)

[45] "Mitch Wishnowsky With the Huge Hit on Broncos Returner," 49ers.com, August 19, 2019 (https://www.49ers.com/video/mitch-wishnowsky-with-the-huge-hit-vs-broncos)

[46] Eric Crocker, Twitter, October 27, 2019 (https://twitter.com/fourth_nine/status/1188561564460171264)

[47] Jose Luis Sanchez III, "49ers GM John Lynch Voted NFL Executive of the Year by PFWA," Sports Illustrated, January 16, 2020 (https://www.si.com/nfl/49ers/news/49ers-john-lynch-voted-nfl-executive-of-year-pfwa)

[48] Lance Zeirlein, "Draft Tracker: Dre Greenlaw Arkansas," NFL.com, undated. (https://www.nfl.com/prospects/dre-greenlaw?id=32194752-4555-7396-3986-bf0359ce742c)

[49] Gerry Dales, Twitter, April 27, 2019 (https://twitter.com/GerryDales/status/1122221336754053126)

[50] Matt Maiocco, "49ers: Linebacker Azeez Al-Shaair," 49ers Insider Podcast, September 3, 2019 (https://art19.com/shows/49ers-insider-podcast/episodes/8e022afd-1785-4dc1-90fa-b6cc6c4dee44)

[51] (https://twitter.com/49ersHub/status/1140979800099528704)

[52] Matt Maiocco, "Trent Taylor has foot surgery, expected back in 4-to-6 weeks," NBC Sports, August 10, 2019 (https://www.nbcsports.com/bayarea/49ers/trent-taylor-has-foot-surgery-expected-back-4-6-weeks)

[53] Jennifer Lee Chan, "49ers' Trent Taylor likely out for 2019 season after suffering setback," NBC Sports, November 9, 2019 (https://www.nbcsports.com/bayarea/49ers/49ers-trent-taylor-likely-out-2019-season-after-suffering-setback)

[54] Jennifer Lee Chan, "49ers' Trent Taylor looks to return in spring after five surgeries," NBC Sports, January 11, 2020 (https://www.nbcsports.com/bayarea/49ers/49ers-trent-taylor-looks-return-spring-after-five-surgeries)

[55] Jessica Kleinschmidt, "49ers-Steelers odds, predictions: Betting lines, picks for NFL Week 3 game," NBC Sports, September 21, 2019 (https://www.nbcsports.com/bayarea/49ers/49ers-steelers-odds-predictions-betting-lines-picks-nfl-week-3-game)

[56] Adam Rank, "Unpopular Opinions: 49ers overhyped; Bills deserve more love," NFL.com, August 5, 2019 (http://www.nfl.com/news/story/0ap3000001039024/article/unpopular-opinions-49ers-overhyped-bills-deserve-more-love)

[57] Jennifer Lee Chan, "Why Richard Sherman wants 49ers' detractors to keep doubting them," NBC Sports, October 8, 2019 (https://www.nbcsports.com/bayarea/49ers/why-richard-sherman-wants-49ers-detractors-keep-doubting-them)

[58] Ted Nguyen, "Super Bowl analysis: Evaluating the 49ers offense vs. the Chiefs defense," The Athletic, January 23, 2020 (https://theathletic.com/1553550/2020/01/23/super-bowl-analysis-evaluating-the-49ers-offense-vs-the-chiefs-defense/)

[59] https://www.youtube.com/watch?v=NaWyoHhL1_Y

[60] Cody Alexander, "Solving the McVay Offense (SB LIII)" MatchQuarters.com, October 10, 2019 (https://matchquarters.com/2019/10/10/solving-the-mcvay-offense-sb-liii/)

[61] Ted Nguyen, "49ers Film Room: The defense's growth is more than just improved talent — Robert Saleh has revamped the scheme," The Athletic, October 16, 2019 (https://theathletic.com/1296227/2019/10/16/49ers-film-room-the-defenses-growth-is-more-than-just-improved-talent-robert-saleh-has-revamped-the-scheme/)

[62] Mark Saltveit, "It's ON! Patriots, 49ers size each other up," Niners Nation, October 24, 2019 (https://www.ninersnation.com/2019/10/24/20929058/its-on-patriots-49ers-size-each-other-up-belichick-shanahan)

[63] Luke Decock, "Panthers expected 49ers' misdirection, but still baffled and bamboozled in blowout," Charlotte Observer, October 27, 2019 (https://www.charlotteobserver.com/sports/spt-columns-blogs/luke-decock/article236686263.html)

[64] Joe Lami (@Joe_Lami), Twitter, October 27, 2019 (https://twitter.com/joe_lami/status/1188627397739835392)

[65] Mark Saltveit, "Shanahan has been five steps ahead of his opponent all season," Niners Nation, October 31, 2019 (https://www.ninersnation.com/2019/10/31/20940626/filmproofing-his-scheme-kyle-shanahan)

[66] Michael Nowels, "Jimmy G, Erin Andrews put 'Feels great, baby' to rest before NFC Championship Game," San Jose Mercury News, January 19, 2020 (https://www.mercurynews.com/2020/01/19/jimmy-g-erin-andrews-put-feels-great-baby-to-rest-before-nfc-championship-game/)

[67] Michael Silver, "San Francisco 49ers fueled by Baker Mayfield's pregame snub," NFL.com, October 8, 2019 (http://www.nfl.com/news/story/0ap3000001063629/article/san-francisco-49ers-fueled-by-baker-mayfields-pregame-snub)

[68] Alaa Abdeldaiem, "Richard Sherman to Apologize to Baker Mayfield Over Handshake Drama," Sports Illustrated, October 9, 2019 (https://www.si.com/nfl/2019/10/09/richard-sherman-apologize-baker-mayfield-handshake)

[69] David Lombardi, "A decade of Richard Sherman: Back in the Super Bowl, the 49ers' star reminisces about a full-circle journey," The Athletic, January 27, 2020 (https://theathletic.com/1562357/2020/01/27/a-decade-of-richard-sherman-back-in-the-super-bowl-the-49ers-star-reminisces-about-a-full-circle-journey/)

[70] Dalton Johnson, "49ers' Richard Sherman says he spoke to Baker Mayfield about handshake," NBC Sports, October 10, 2019 (https://www.nbcsports.com/bayarea/49ers/49ers-richard-sherman-says-he-spoke-baker-mayfield-about-handshake)

[71] Sam Monson, "49ers' Richard Sherman selected as PFF's top coverage defender for 2019", Pro Football Focus, January 22, 2020 (https://www.pff.com/news/nfl-49ers-richard-sherman-pff-best-coverage-defender-2019)

[72] Jose Luis Sanchez III, "49ers' Emmanuel Moseley has Solidified the Cornerback Position," Sports Illustrated, January 23, 2020 (https://www.si.com/nfl/49ers/news/49ers-emmanuel-moseley-solidified-cornerback-position)

[73] Greg Bishop, "This 49ers Team Is Super Bowl–Bound on the Backs of Their Defense and ... Raheem Mostert," Sports Illustrated, January 20, 2020 (https://www.si.com/nfl/2020/01/20/san-francisco-49ers-defense-raheem-mostert-nfl-playoffs-nfc-championship)

[74] Ted Nguyen, "49ers Film Room: Mistakes and the 'human cheat code' spoiled the plan to slow down Baltimore's Lamar Jackson," The Athletic, December 4, 2019 (https://theathletic.com/1428568/2019/12/04/49ers-film-room-mistakes-and-the-human-cheat-code-spoiled-the-plan-to-slow-down-baltimores-lamar-jackson/)

[75] Ted Nguyen, "49ers Film Room: How the Falcons broke tendencies and made things uncomfortable on both sides of the ball", The Athletic, December 18, 2019 (https://theathletic.com/1469836/2019/12/18/49ers-film-room-how-the-falcons-broke-tendencies-and-made-things-uncomfortable-on-both-sides-of-the-ball/)

[76] Ted Nguyen, "49ers analysis: The defense needs to do a better job of taking away opponents' strengths early in the game," The Athletic, December 26, 2019 (https://theathletic.com/1485619/2019/12/26/49ers-analysis-the-defense-needs-to-do-a-better-job-of-taking-away-opponents-strengths-early-in-the-game/)

[77] Ted Nguyen, "Super Bowl analysis: Evaluating the 49ers offense vs. the Chiefs defense," The Athletic, January 23, 2020 (https://theathletic.com/1553550/2020/01/23/super-bowl-analysis-evaluating-the-49ers-offense-vs-the-chiefs-defense/)

[78] Official NFL highlight on Twitter, January 11, 2020. (https://twitter.com/NFL/status/1216118238016204800)

[79] Jennifer Lee Chan, "Jimmy Garoppolo's big pancake block energizes 49ers in win vs. Vikings," NBC Sports, January 11, 2020 (https://www.nbcsports.com/bayarea/49ers/jimmy-garoppolos-big-pancake-block-energizes-49ers-win-vs-vikings)

[80] ibid

[81] Albert Breer, the MMQB, January 20, 2020 (https://www.si.com/nfl/2020/01/20/nfl-playoffs-super-bowl-liv-49ers-chiefs-patrick-mahomes-kyle-shanahan-mmqb)

[82] Video of George Kittle on Jennifer Lee Chan's Twitter feed, January 31, 2020 (https://twitter.com/jenniferleechan/status/1223341917947252736)

[83] "Draft Tracker: Dre Greenlaw," NFL.com, (https://www.nfl.com/prospects/dre-greenlaw?id=32194752-4555-7396-3986-bf0359ce742c)

[84] ibid

[85] Video of George Kittle on Jennifer Lee Chan's Twitter feed, January 31, 2020 (https://twitter.com/jenniferleechan/status/1223341917947252736)

[86] Jennifer Lee Chan, "49ers ready to show Chiefs, world how violent, physical they can be," NBCSports, January 30, 2020 (https://www.nbcsports.com/bayarea/49ers/49ers-ready-show-chiefs-world-how-violent-physical-they-can-be)

[87] Patrick Holloway, "Emmanuel Sanders on the 2019 49ers: "I love every single one of these guys. I love everybody from the general manager to the head coach," Niners Nation, January 28, 2020 (https://www.ninersnation.com/2020/1/28/21111359/super-bowl-liv-interviews-emmanuel-sanders-love-brother-hood-steelers-broncos-ben-roethlisberger)

[88] Jennifer Lee Chan, "49ers ready to show Chiefs, world how violent, physical they can be," NBCSports, January 30, 2020 (https://www.nbcsports.com/bayarea/49ers/49ers-ready-show-chiefs-world-how-violent-physical-they-can-be)

[89] Greg Bishop, "This 49ers Team Is Super Bowl–Bound on the Backs of Their Defense and ... Raheem Mostert," Sports Illustrated, January 20, 2020 (https://www.si.com/nfl/2020/01/20/san-francisco-49ers-defense-raheem-mostert-nfl-playoffs-nfc-championship)

[90] Seth Wickersham, "Behind the 49ers' Super Bowl return, two men who changed everything," ESPN.com, January 22, 2020 (https://www.espn.com/nfl/story/_/id/28531499/behind-49ers-super-bowl-return-two-men-changed-everything)